Ohio High S(

Training Met

By
Chuck Bridgman

ISBN13: 9781461068129

Visit our web site at www.highschooldistancerunning.com

Printed in the United States of America

Third Edition Prolog

What To Do On Race Day and the American Kenyans
The previous two editions of this book left off at tapering for the big race. Now we have what to do on race day. We spent a lot of time on analyzing past races of the mile and 1500m, plus we've interviewed some of the great ones that broke 4 minutes in high school – Marty Liquori, Tim Danielson, Alan Webb and high school teammates of Jim Ryun. And from this we've created the Three Laws of Racing the Mile. Hope you enjoy and find beneficial Marty and Jim's high school workouts.

Chuck Bridgman
12/2015

Second Edition Prolog

More Reason To Believe
What prompted me to publish a second edition of this book was a talk I had with Don Neff, the father of the 2008 and 2009 1600m State Champ. Don Neff told me I should interview his son, Danny Neff, who is attending the University of Georgia. Danny told me he read this book the winter of his junior year. He followed its recommendations and went on to win back to back Division I State 1600m titles his junior and senior years. Wow, as they say in the rock and roll song "this really blew my mind." That's Real Reason To Believe baby!

Danny's profile is included in this edition and as expected his training and race preparation follow the norm set by the previous state champs. A great living example of "you too can do it."

Chuck Bridgman
1/2011

SPORTS

Panthers chew 'em up

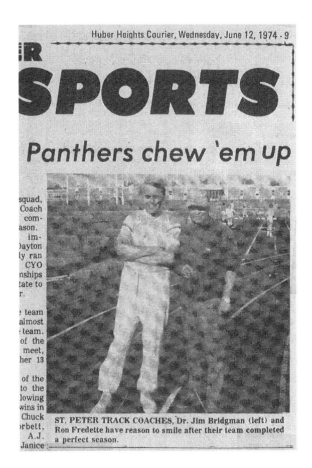

squad,
Coach
com-
ason.
im-
Dayton
ly ran
CYO
nships
tate to
r.

e team
almost
team.
of the
meet,
her 13

of the
to the
lowing
wins in
Chuck
rbett,
A.J.
Janice

ST. PETER TRACK COACHES, Dr. Jim Bridgman (left) and Ron Fredette have reason to smile after their team completed a perfect season.

To my dad and the other men of St Peter's Parish.   They built a church, raised their families, won the cold war and on the weekends took their kids out to the athletic fields and showed them how to compete and win.

Contents

*"Don't ever step onto the track
unless you plan on winning."*

1949 Iowa High School Men's State Half Mile Champion

*In the race all the runners run, but only one gets the prize.
Run in such a way as to get the prize.*
Paul, 1 Corinthians 9:24

Introduction

"Hey coach, what does it take to win state?"

It was my first day back coaching and a young man on my team asked me this simple question, to which I did not have a good, clear and concise answer. It seems natural that a coach should know exactly what it takes to win state. There are coaches who were themselves high school state mile champions and others that have coached one if not more state mile champions. But nowhere is there a handbook describing the exact workouts and requirements needed to win the Division I State 1600m race.

The Ohio State High School Athletic Association has been awarding the mile and 1600m state championship since 1911. If this many runners have won the race, then what it takes to win the race should not be a mystery.

So herein lies the purpose of this book - to document what the winners of the state mile and 1600m race did in order to win.

The Process

The quest to find the answer started with some basic conversations with runners that I knew and who had won the state mile. These informal discussions took place at meets and other locations where I would run into these acquaintances. After two or three of these informal interviews I started to format the questions and document the answers. I soon ran out of winners that I personally knew. The next step was to get a list of state winners and find the runners that had set a new meet record, won multiple years, or had a significant impact with winning the race. Once I tracked down these people I conducted phone interviews.

For these interviews I created a list of approximately two dozen questions geared towards finding the winners' trends and methods rather than trying to document daily workouts. Almost everyone knows how to run a hard quarter mile repeat workout, but the questions go beyond the standard interval workouts to determine the critical as well as the noncritical factors that are essential to winning the Division I State 1600m.

Upon conclusion of the interviews the details were compiled into spreadsheets and logs. The 17 separate interviews with their individual answers were then compared against each other. From this matrix the individual categories of interview questions were cataloged as relevant and irrelevant along with minimum requirements.

The final step was to take the relevant and minimum requirements along with the most common training method, and create a season-long practice routine populated with the workouts.

3

One Mile vs. 1600 Meters

In 1980, the Ohio High School Athletic Association changed the race distance from one mile to 1600 meters. The difference is that the mile is 30.624 feet longer than the 1600m and the 1600 meters is equal to 0.9942 miles. Using the multiplier of 0.9942 on the mile time, the following table converts the mile time to the 1600m time.

Mile	1600m
4:00.00	3:58.61
4:05.00	4:03.58
4:10.00	4:08.55
4:15.00	4:13.52
4:20.00	4:18.49
4:25.00	4:23.46
4:30.00	4:28.43

This book slips between yards and meters distances as runners interviewed talk about quarter mile repeats one moment and 400m repeats the next. Times listed for the mile are not converted to the 1600m unless noted.

Ohio High School State Mile Champions

The Records

Now the focus shifts to the winners of the mile and 1600m. The following tables contain the overall list of the winners from 1964 – 2009 (pg 9), the list of Record Setters (pg 11) and the list of the fastest recorded times (pg 12).

Ohio High School Mile And 1600 State Winners Division I

Year	Winner	Time	School
1964	**Rickey Poole**	4:19.6 Record	Dayton Jefferson Twp High School
1965	Tom Schoenig	4:18.1 Record	Amherst Steele High School
1966	Bill Johnson	4:18.5	Akron South High School
1967	Wes Brock	4:17.9 Record	Toledo Libbey High School
1968	**Dave Wottle**	**4:20.2**	**Canton Lincoln High School**
1969	Reggie Mcafee	4:08.5 Record	Cincinnati Courter Tech High School
1970	**Bill Beaty**	**4:13.8**	**Lancaster High School**
1971	Mike Burley	4:14.1	Berea High School
1972	**Ron Addison**	**4:13.5**	**Cleveland Rhodes High School**
1973	Marc Hunter	4:17.6	Brunswick High School
1974	Marc Hunter	4:15.1	Brunswick High School
1975	Kevin Ryan	4:14.7	Cleveland St Joseph Academy High School
1976	Robert Williamson	4:16.4	Maple Heights High School
1977	**Tom Rapp**	**4:13.2**	**Trotwood-Madison High School**
1978	**Alan Scharsu**	**4:13.1**	**Austintown-Fitch High School**
1979	**John Ziska**	**4:11.2**	**Lancaster High School**
1980	Mike Hallabrin	4:07.7	Mansfield Malabar High School
1981	**Clark Haley**	**4:14.1**	**Lancaster High School**
1982	Dean Monske	4:11.34	Toledo De Vilbiss High School
1983	**Rollie Hudson**	**4:14.98**	**Cleveland Heights High School**
1984	**Rollie Hudson**	**4:11.89**	**Cleveland Heights High School**
1985	Kevin Sheward	4:11.32	Canton Mc Kinley High School
1986	**Mark Croghan**	**4:10.78**	**Greensburg Green High School**
1987	**Bob Kennedy**	**4:10.49**	**Westerville North High School**
1988	**Bob Kennedy**	**4:05.13 Record**	**Westerville North High School**
1989	Shawn Norman	4:12.58	Canton Timken High School
1990	**Darrell Huges**	**4:12.38**	**Galloway Westland High School**

6

1991	**Darell Hughes**	**4:11.58**	**Galloway Westland High School**
1992	Jeff Hojnacki	4:13.32	Solon High School
1993	Jim Bournes	4:18.85	Toledo Whitmer High School
1994	Doug Bockenstette	4:10.14	Cincinnati La Salle High School
1995	Dean Fulmer	4:15.33	Cincinnati La Salle High School
1996	Adam Smith	4:18.09	Hudson High School
1997	Adam Thomas Jr.	4:15.76	Fairfield High School
1998	Chris Estwanik	4:12.50	Dublin Coffman High School
1999	**Mason Ward**	**4:12.04**	**Cincinnati Colerain High School**
2000	**Mason Ward**	**4:07**	**Cincinnati Colerain High School**
2001	Jesse Rhodenbaugh	4:08.70	Oxford Talawanda High School
2002	Allen Bader	4:14.37	Cincinnati La Salle High School
2003	**Jeff See**	**4:06.81**	**Middletown High School**
2004	**Jeff See**	**4:14.00**	**Middletown High School**
2005	**Jeff See**	**4:11.20**	**Middletown High School**
2006	Max Hiltner	4:17.26	Wadsworth High School
2007	**Jake Edwards**	**4:09.89**	**Delaware Hayes High School**
2008	**Danny Neff**	**4:15.9**	**Vandalia Butler High School**
2009	**Danny Neff**	**4:10.6**	**Vandalia Butler High School**

List supplied by OHSAA and some times from Dayton Daily News. Interviewed runners shown in bold. Times with 100ths of a second are automated times.

What Time Does It Take To Win

The average time needed to win the 1600m in the state division I race since 1964 is 4:12.73. This average time includes converting the mile to 1600m times. Average time needed for winning since 1970 is 4:12.28. Below is the table for average times needed to win for the separate decades.

Decade	Time
1970s	4:12.71
1980's	4:11.03
1990's	4:14.00
2000's	4:11.16

Ohio High School State Mile Champions

Ohio High School Mile and 1600 Meter Record Setters

Mile Record	1600m Record	Runner	School	Date	Location
05:15.0		Bush	Wellington	6/3/1894	Elyria
05:09.2		Crandall	Elyria	6/9/1895	Elyria
5:05 ¾		Romio	Findlay	5/31/1902	Findlay
05:00.0		Saxton	Tol. Central	5/28/1904	Oberlin
04:56.2		McWatters	Clev. Central	5/31/1905	Cleveland
04:56.2		Bowman	Clev. Central	5/31/1905	Cleveland
04:50.0		Carl Deeter	Dayt. Steele	6/3/1905	Granville
04:41.0		Paul Schoenfeldt	Tol. Central	6/3/1911	Cleveland
04:40.2		Hainsworth	Oberlin	5/25/1913	Cleveland
04:38.2		John Schubert	Col. East	5/23/1914	Columbus
04:36.2		Louis Cody	East Clev. Shaw	5/17/1915	Pittsburgh, PA
04:34.3		Irving Heipel	Tol. Scott	5/26/1917	Columbus
04:32.9		Harvey Smith	Lakewood	5/24/1930	Columbus
04:32.0		Sharon McMullen	Ak. Garfield	early 1932	
04:28.5		Sharon McMullen	Ak. Garfield	5/28/1932	Columbus
04:24.5		Bob Curtis	East Clev. Shaw	5/30/1936	Columbus
04:23.0		Jim Davis	unat, Akron	Jun-58	Berea
04:20.0		George Brose	Dayt. Belmont	5/19/1961	Dayton
04:19.7		Andy Schramm	Deer Park	4/27/1962	Lockland
04:18.0		Andy Schramm	Deer Park	5/12/1962	Oxford
04:15.4		Steve Korinchak	Clev. Rhodes	5/22/1965	Mansfield
04:15.3		Wes Brock	Tol. Libbey	5/15/1966	Maumee
04:13.3		Reggie McAfee	Cin. Courter Tech	May-69	
04:08.5		Reggie McAfee	Cin. Courter Tech	5/24/1969	Columbus
04:05.9		Ron Addison	Clev. Rhodes	6/10/1972	Baton Rouge, LA
	04:29.0	Joel Albers	Clev. Heights	4/22/1978	Eastlake
	04:19.0	Chris Burke	Mayfield	5/13/1978	Eastlake
	04:09.9	John Zishka	Lancaster	4/28/1979	Bellaire
04:05.8		John Zishka	Lancaster	May-80	Chillicothe
	04:06.8	John Zishka	Lancaster	5/24/1980	Gahanna
04:03.9		John Zishka	Lancaster	6/14/1980	Sacramento, CA
	04:06.8	Bob Kennedy	Westerville North	5/21/1988	Columbus
	04:05.1	Bob Kennedy	Westerville North	6/4/1988	Columbus
4:03.33		Sam Borchers	Yellow Springs	6/15/2007	Greensboro, NC

List compiled by Craig Whitmore.

Fastest Mile and 1600 Meter Recorded Races

1600m Time	Runner	School	Year
4:01.9*	Sam Borchers	Yellow Springs	2007
4:02.4*	John Zishka	Lancaster	1980
4:04.5*	Ron Addison	Clev. Rhodes	1972
04:05.1	Bob Kennedy	Westerville North	1988
4:04.6*	Jeff See	Middletown	2003
4:06.0*	Mason Ward	unattached (Cincinnati)	2000
4:07.1*	Reggie McAfee	Cin. Courter Tech	1969
4:07.1*	Darrell Hughes	Galloway Westland	1991
04:07.7	Mike Hallabrin	Mans. Malabar	1980
04:08.0	Scott Fry	Sandusky Perkins	1985
4:08.2*	Alan Scharsu	Yng. Austintown-Fitch	1978
4:08.4*	Tom Rapp	Trotwood-Madison	1977
4:08.6*	Todd Saul	Clayton Northmont	1981
04:08.7	Jesse Rodenbaugh	Oxford Talawanda	2001
04:09.1	Rob Myers	Lancaster Fairfield Union	1999
04:09.5	Christian Nichols	Hilliard Davidson	2003
04:10.1	Jerry Claunch	Liberty Twp Lakota East	2000
04:10.1	Doug Bockenstette	Cin. LaSalle	1994
4:10.6*	Chris Kollar	Strongsville	2003
04:10.8	Mark Croghan	Greensburg Green	1986
04:10.8	Samuel Borchers	Yellow Springs	2007
04:11.2	Chris Lemon	Tol. St. John's	2007
04:11.3	Kevin Sheward	Cant. McKinley	1985
04:11.3	Dean Monske	Tol. DeVilbiss	1982
04:11.5	Jason Mueller	Shelby	1999
04:11.5	Steve Padgett	Cin. LaSalle	2000

Mile time reduced by 0.58% to get an equivalent 1600m time.

List compiled by Craig Whitmore.

Ohio High School State Mile Champions   www.highschooldistancerunning.com

Ohio High School State Mile Champions

Interviewing the Runners

When I first started this project it was nothing more than gathering some specific details from a few runners I knew on how they ran during high school. My intent was to find some common denominator's of state mile and 1600m champions. In the beginning I had a list of questions that I thought were relevant in determining what was required to win a state mile title. However, as I started interviewing the first few runners, my list of questions was modified with input from the runners and then standardized for the rest of the interviews.

Interviewing these runners was a great pleasure. Without exception, every single one of the runners I called up, out of the blue, returned my call and offered their time and information freely. The runners spent anywhere from 30 minutes to two hours on the phone with me. They answered my questions while they were traveling on business, watching the kids or even during the dinner hour. I would call them up introduce myself and schedule a future interview call with them. I would call back for the interview at scheduled time and they would have their scrapbooks out, workout logs and even offer names and contacts of other runners that won the title with recommendations that I call. One of the double title winners, Mason Ward from Colerain, was in the active military and I was able to interview him before he shipped out to Afghanistan. Olympians like Mark Croghan and Bob Kennedy showed no hesitation revealing their high school workout routines. Calling and interviewing my own childhood idol, Dave Wottle, caused some hesitation on my part. His 1972 gold-medal performance in Munich was burned into my memory and my own state titles were run mimicking Dave. I would run in last place for the first half of the race and on the bell lap imagine that the final runners I passed were the same Kenyans and Russian that Dave beat to win the 800m gold medal.

The interview questions and answers along with narrative from the runners are documented in the following chapters. I tried to keep out the runners individual thoughts and theories on training and stay with just the details and facts. I also limited the documented responses to only what happened in high school and removed any details of post-high school running.

1960's

Ninty miles an hour, girl, is the speed I drive.
You tell me it's alright, you don't mind a little pain.
You say you just want me to take you for a ride.
Crosstown Traffic - Jimi Hendrix

Ricky Poole
Jefferson High School - 1964
"Can do, should do, will do. That was my mantra. Track was my ticket to college and I put a big 4:20 on the wall in my bedroom."

1964, one year before Jim Ryun would break the four-minute mile as a high school runner. Ohio State University would replace the cinder track in Ohio Stadium with an all weather surface, and Bob Schul from West Milton, Ohio would win the Olympic 5000m gold medal in Tokyo. That same year Ricky Poole would be the first high school miler to break 4:20 at the Ohio State high school track championships. Over the next seven years that state mile record would be lowered five times.

The last Saturday in May, 1964 Ricky Pool from Jefferson High School outside of Dayton Ohio would usher in the era of fast high school milers in the State of Ohio. Poole consecrated the new all weather track in Ohio Stadium with a 4:19 mile that day, a state meet record. Two hours later he ripped off a 1:55.7 half-mile for another state record.

Starting Out

Ricky Pool started running competitively in seventh-grade. In high school he ran cross country and track all four years. The fall of his freshman year, he competed in cross country and freshman football. During the winter Ricky played basketball for Jefferson high. At 6' 1, Ricky was a standout on a very good varsity basketball team and his senior year he was offered several basketball scholarships by Division II colleges.

Spring Training

Ricky ran throughout the summer of his high school years, this included running long road miles on Sundays. During the track season Ricky ran twice a day. In the morning, he ran a few miles on the road, followed in the afternoon by a track workout. A typical week during the track season would consist of a dual meet on Tuesday and an interval workout Wednesday and Thursday on Jefferson's cinder track. These track workouts typically consisted of quarter mile repeats. Ricky would run eight quarters at approximately 62 second pace.

13

Ohio High School State Mile Champions

Training throughout the track season consisted of a very modern, for the time, routine of running more mileage in the early part of the season, followed by intervals in the midseason. These intervals became faster with less rest between them as the season progressed.

Ricky also did structured weight training three times a week during the season.

Tapering and Race Day

At the end of the season coming into the district and state meet, Ricky did no tapering. Workouts stayed at the same effort level as earlier in the season. Although Ricky did not reduced the intensity of his workouts, he and his coach were careful not to overwork prior to the big races. So while Ricky's workouts did not decrease in effort, neither did they increase.

Race day, Ricky would warm up 60 minutes before the gun with some light jogging and stretching. This race strategy consisted of going out front and staying there. Ricky did not have a set pace to follow, he was a classic front runner.

Ricky Poole Stats and Traits and Habits

Started running at age.	13
Eating the night before a race.	NA
Eating the day of a race.	NA
Running on Sundays.	Yes
Running cross country.	Yes
Running after the cross county season.	No
Miles per week during the track season.	45
Miles per week during the winter.	NA
Ran indoor track.	No
Ran weekday dual meets during track season.	Yes – one every week
Number of interval workouts during the week.	Dual meet - plus one
Height	6'0"
Weight	150
Fastest mile was run at State.	Yes – 4:19
Doubled up at State Meet.	Yes
Did weight lifting.	Yes
Stretching	Yes
Calisthenics	No
Tapering for week of state.	No
Eating race day	Yes
Running twice a day	Yes
Cross training	No
Fastest 800	1:58
Fastest 400	53
Training Method	Igloi – Interval

Dave Wottle
Canton Lincoln - 1968

"I was a one season athlete. I didn't run a lot of base miles in high school. I think that's why I progressed so rapidly in college"

As we scanned down the list of state mile winners we're not surprised to see the name Dave Wottle for the 1968 winner, because four years later in Munich, 1972 Dave Wottle would win the 800m gold-medal in one of the most dramatic races in Olympic track and field history. What is surprising is that Dave captured the state mile title with the most minimal work of any of our runners.

Starting Out

Dave started competitive running his freshman year in high school at Canton Lincoln High School. Dave's high school did not have a cross country program and he only ran track. The track team started training in February for the spring season.

Dave played football, basketball and baseball up until his sophomore year in high school.

He ran throughout the winter his senior year, logging about 25 miles a week. That winter, Dave's track coach scheduled a couple of indoor meets. These consisted of traveling to Pittsburgh and running in the TSTCA indoor championship on a dirt track. At this Pittsburgh meet Dave placed fifth in the mile with a 4:51 and then won the half-mile.

Spring Training

During the spring track season, Dave's mileage was not high volume. If he ran 5 miles one day it was considered a lot of distance. The weekly workout schedule for the spring track season consisted of dual meets on Tuesday and Thursday and workouts on Monday Wednesday and Friday. During the track season Dave had two meets every week and he believes that he raced himself into shape during the track season. Dave usually ran the mile, the half-mile and the mile relay in every meet.

Track workouts were on Don Scott Field in Akron which was an asphalt track. These workouts consisted of 440 and 220 repeats with a few half-mile repeats and not anything longer. Dave mentioned that the

16

training was not a sophisticated program. His coach was Jeff Daniels from Muskegon College who was a sprinting coach.

Dave did weightlifting at home and also at Don Scott Field starting his freshman year. This weight lifting was also supplemented with sit-ups and push-ups.

Tapering and Race Day

Because of Dave's minimalist training efforts, it is not surprising to find that he tapered only a small amount at the end of the season. On race day, before the gun Dave did a half-mile jog, some light stretching and a few strides.

Ohio High School State Mile Champions

Dave Wottle Stats and Traits and Habits

Started running at age.	14
Eating the night before a race.	No Spec
Eating the day of a race.	Yes
Running on Sundays.	No
Running cross country.	No
Running after the cross county season.	No
Miles per week during the track season.	25
Miles per week during the winter.	25
Ran indoor track.	Yes – 2 Meets
Ran weekday dual meets during track season.	Yes – Tues
Number of interval workouts during the week.	One
Height	5'11"
Weight	130
Fastest mile was run at State.	Yes – 4:20
Doubled up at State Meet.	No
Did weight lifting.	Yes
Stretching	Yes
Calisthenics	Yes
Tapering for week of state.	Yes
Running twice a day	No
Cross training	No
Fastest 800	NA
Fastest 400	NA
Training Method	Intervals

1970's

Baby take my hand,
Don't fear the Reaper.
We'll be able to fly,
Don't fear the Reaper.
Baby I'm your man.
Don't Fear The Reaper - Blue Oyster Cult

Bill Beaty
Lancaster - 1970

"I ran the first half in 1:57 hoping to pull the kick out of the other runners."

1970 started a new decade for Ohio high school milers. A sub 4:20 was no longer good enough to win state. The year before in 1969 Reggie McAfee from Courter Tech in Cincinnati knocked almost 10 seconds off the state record. Running a 4:09, Reggie set a new benchmark and from that day on if you wanted to win state in the big school division mile you better be ready to run around 4:10.

Lancaster High School, just south of Columbus, is the first school in the state to have three separate state mile champions. 1970 saw the first of the great Lancaster milers, Bill Beaty, win the state mile title.

Starting Out

Bill started running competitively as a freshman in high school. He ran track all four years and ran cross country his sophomore, junior and senior years. Bill was the state cross country champion both his junior and senior years. His cross country training consisted almost exclusively of long mileage. However, towards the end of the cross country season, his coach would insert some speed workouts. One classic workout was the two-man 10 mile relay. This consisted of two runners alternating quarter-mile intervals for 40 laps. Bill and his teammate would run each one these quarters under 70 seconds.

During Bill's junior year, he qualified for state in the mile and two mile with a qualifying time of 9:20 for the two mile. However, the next week at state he warmed up too much in the heat and failed to win either the mile or two mile. He learned a valuable lesson that junior year and did not repeat the mistake his senior year. Bill's senior year he qualified for both the mile and two-mile. His two mile time was 9:15, the fastest qualifying time in the state, but he did not double up at the state meet, and ran only the mile, winning with a 4:13.

Spring Training

After cross country season, Bill continued running four to five days a week. These runs consisted of road runs anywhere from five to 10 miles. He would log approximately 35 to 50 miles per week during the winter. Bill ran three to four indoor meets during the winter. He did very little speed work for these indoor races, mostly relying on his road mile workouts.

Track season consisted of running one or two interval workouts during the week, usually consisting of mile or half-mile repeats. Bill would have a two-mile warmup and a two-mile warm down. He did these interval workouts during the week, usually Wednesday or Thursday. These workouts were run not on a track, but at a local park. Monday was typically a hard distance run day, followed by a dual-meet on Tuesday.

Bill religiously used a stopwatch during all his runs. He would run a four mile workout at a 4:50 mile pace. The next time he ran that same four mile workout he would try to better that 4:50 mile pace. Weekly mileage during the track season was 50 to 70 miles per week.

Tapering and Race Day

The week of the state meet Bill stopped all speed work and only ran hard distance runs. Miles were reduced 20% down to 40 - 50 miles for the week of the State Meet. Race day routine consisted of warming up 45 minutes before the gun. Bill would start by jogging a mile then 15 minutes before the gun he would run 10 to 12 strides. Eating on race day consisted of a light breakfast of toast.

Bill ran a 4:10 in the district meet the week before state. The following week Bill won the state mile in 4:13. His slower state time was due to his concern about a very good miler from Dayton named Bobby Reed. Reed had 49 second quarter mile speed and Bill's race strategy was to go out fast and pull the kick out of Bobby before the end of the race. Bill did this with a 57 second first-quarter mile and then came through the half that 1:57. The strategy worked as Bobby Reed stayed with Bill the first three laps of the race and then faded away on the bell lap.

Bill Beaty Stats and Traits and Habits

Started running at age.	15
Eating the night before a race.	Pasta
Eating the day of a race.	Toast
Running on Sundays.	Yes
Running cross country.	Yes
Running after the cross county season.	Yes – No break
Miles per week during the track season.	60
Miles per week during the winter.	45
Ran indoor track.	Yes
Ran weekday dual meets during track season.	Yes
Number of interval workouts during the week.	Yes 2 days
Height	6'0"
Weight	135
Fastest mile was run at State.	No
Doubled up at State Meet.	No
Did weight lifting.	No
Stretching.	No
Calisthenics.	No
Tapering for week of state.	Yes
Running twice a day.	NA
Cross training.	No
Fastest 800.	1:58
Fastest 400.	NA
Training Method	Lydiard

23

₁n Addison
₊veland Rhodes - 1972

In the summer of 1972, Steve Prefontaine was running in the Munich Olympics and Ron Addison of Cleveland Rhodes High School would be clocking the second fastest mile ever by an Ohio high school runner, a 4:05.9, in Baton Rogue LA.

Starting Out

Ron started competitively running track and cross country as a sophomore in high school. Ron's fastest mile as a sophomore was 4:22. As a junior, his fastest mile of the year was 4:14.9 which placed him second at the state meet. Ron did not participate in other organized high school sports besides running. However, he consistently played pickup football, baseball and basketball.

Ron ran cross country his sophomore, junior and senior years and he ran through the winter his junior and senior years. He consistently ran 10 miles a day, not super hard runs, but good tempo runs. Ron ran indoor track during the winter and trained 50 miles a week during the indoor season. He had a fairly full indoor track meet schedule. During the winter indoor season Ron would do some interval workouts. His high school, Cleveland Rhodes, was built in the 1930's and had an indoor dirt track in the basement. This dirt track was an irregular shape with some 90 degree turns.

Ron won the state mile his senior year with a time of 4:13. This was not his fastest time of the year because that first Saturday in June the OSU track was very hot. He had run 4:11 the week before at a cooler District Meet, and even earlier in the season he had been timed at 4:10 in a 4 x 1 mile relay. Ron doubled up at State his senior year and also ran a half-mile. His half-mile time at state was also not his fastest, again due to the heat. He ran a 1:58 in the 880 at state and placed fourth. Ron's fastest two mile on the track was 9:06. He also won the cross country state meet his senior year

Ron was 5'9" and 125 lbs. during his senior track season. He did no weightlifting or any calisthenics during his high school training but stretched before every practice.

Spring Training

Ron's typical training during the track season was a 6 to 8 mile run on Sunday, intervals on Monday, a dual meet on Tuesday, a mid mileage run on Wednesday, Thursday would be another interval workout day, then short easy mileage on Friday before a Saturday meet.

On Mondays, Ron ran longer intervals consisting of miles, three quarters of a mile and half-miles. Thursday's intervals usually consisted of a shorter distance such as quarter miles. The length of intervals became shorter later in the season.

Tapering and Race Day

Ron worked very hard up until the state week, then knocked back the mileage and workouts to half of what they were. Ron worked through the sectional and district meets before the state meet only tapering for the state meet itself.

Ron did not have any special meals the night before meets. He does mention that his mother was from the south and there was a lot of gravy and biscuits and mashed potatoes, a diet heavy with carbohydrates. The day of the race Ron would only make sure that his last meal was a full four hours before this race. If the race was a late afternoon or evening he would eat his breakfast at the lunch hour.

Ron's race day routine consisted of trying to stay out of the sun and limiting his activities until 45 minutes before the race, trying to relax. Starting 45 minutes before the gun, Ron would jog a couple miles, do some strides, stretch out and jog a little more.

Ohio High School State Mile Champions

Ron Addison Stats and Traits and Habits

Started running at age.	16
Eating the night before a race.	No spec
Eating the day of a race.	Standard breakfast
Running on Sundays.	Yes – 7 mi.
Running cross country.	Yes
Running after the cross county season.	Yes – Two week break
Miles per week during the track season.	60
Miles per week during the winter.	50
Ran indoor track.	Yes
Ran weekday dual meets during track season.	NA
Number of interval workouts during the week.	Yes - 2 days
Height	5'9"
Weight	125
Fastest mile was run at State.	No
Doubled up at State Meet.	Yes
Did weight lifting.	No
Stretching	Yes
Calisthenics	No
Tapering for week of state.	Yes – one week
Eating race day	Yes
Running twice a day	NA
Cross training	No
Fastest 800	1:55
Fastest 400	NA
Training Method	Igloi – Track Intervals

Tom Rapp
Trotwood High School - 1977

"I got away with murder over and over and over again. God must of protected me. I had a day where my knees really hurt and I ran through it. And the next day I ran 10 hard."

In Eugene, Oregon, in the 1980's there were six former Ohio high school track champions running together - Tom Rapp was one these. The others were John Zishka, Allan Scharsu, Kevin Ryan, Tom Byers and Ron Addison. Tom Byers was the only runner that did not win the state mile, although he won the state half-mile.

Starting Out
Tom Rapp started running track in seventh grade in Trotwood Ohio, a northwest suburb of Dayton Ohio.

Tom ran cross country all four years while he was at Trotwood High School. His senior year between cross country and track he ran throughout the winter and took very little time off, only a few days of no running. Tom ran 65 miles a week during this winter training period.

During the winter of Tom's senior year, he ran four indoor track meets. He ran no hard interval workouts and did not peak for these winter indoor meets. His senior year, Tom worked under the guidance of Bob Schul, the 1964 5000m gold medal winner from Milton Union, Ohio. Schul's practice method consisted of focused interval workouts and Tom was always doing some type of race pace or faster workout consistently through the track season.

Tom considers himself as not having a lot of foot speed. He states that if there was a 200m race he was sure to be the slowest guy. Tom believes, as does Bob Schul, that if you do enough speed work you can start to overcome slow foot speed.

Spring Training

Tom's coach at Trotwwod high school was Tom Snare, a standout runner at Miami University and a great motivator. Snare followed the Igloi methodology doing interval workouts three days a week on Monday, Tuesday and Thursday. Friday before meet was always very easy, just a few strides. Tom never ran hard practices close to a meet and ran very few weekday dual meets in track. Tom ran more mileage at the beginning of the track season and ran more speed and fewer miles towards the end of the season.

Ohio High School State Mile Champions

Tom's coach in high school was very big on keeping a running log and as a consequence Tom kept one during his high school years.

Tapering and race Day

The week of State Tom had a "short and sweet" workout schedule that consisted of 200m repeats. Mileage came down the week of state from 45 to 30 miles a week. He tapered very little the two weeks before the week of state.

Tom did weightlifting throughout the preseason and early-season, two or three times a week but stopped lifting towards the end of the season.

Tom had no special diet the night before a race - just a pasta dinner. The day of the race was just a couple pieces of French toast for breakfast, no acidic or dairy products.

Tom's race routine before the gun was modified after his sophomore year when he totally blew up at State by doing too much prerace activity. Consequently, his junior and senior years he just stayed under the stadium, played cards, relaxed and took it easy before his race. This easier prerace routine had Tom warming up 60 minutes before the gun, jogging a mile and doing some strides and stretching.

Tom won the State mile his senior year but did not run his fastest mile at the State meet. He ran a 4:11 the week before state meet, and then ran 4:13 at state. Tom was confident going in the state as he had a seven second faster time than the next closest qualifier for state. His race strategy for state was to run even pace laps. However someone went out fast the first quarter and Tom followed him and they came through the first quarter at 61 seconds.

Tom did not double up at the state meet. In fact, he rarely doubled up in meets throughout the season. It was only his senior year that the State High School Athletic Association allowed runners to run the mile and the two mile in the same meet. Tom liked to put all his efforts into one race. He did not like to get ready for two races or have the mental burden of a second race in his mind during the first race. Tom wanted to be 100% ready to win one race and run it as hard as he possibly could. He did not want the feeling of being handicapped running the second race.

Tom Rapp Stats and Traits and Habits

Started running at age.	13
Eating the night before a race.	Pasta
Eating the day of a race.	Toast
Running on Sundays.	Yes – 7 to 10 mi.
Running cross country.	Yes
Running after the cross county season.	Yes – No break
Miles per week during the track season.	45
Miles per week during the winter.	60
Ran indoor track.	Yes – 4 meets
Ran weekday dual meets during track season.	No
Number of interval workouts during the week.	Yes - 3 days
Height	6'1"
Weight	145
Fastest mile was run at State.	No – 4:13
Doubled up at State Meet.	No
Did weight lifting.	No
Stretching	Yes
Calisthenics	No
Tapering for week of state.	Yes – one week
Eating race day	Yes
Running twice a day	NA
Cross training	No
Fastest 800	1:58
Fastest 400	53
Training Method	Igloi – Track Intervals

29

Ohio High School State Mile Champions

Alan Scharsu
Youngstown Austintown-Fitch High School - 1978
"We never did any track workouts."

Starting Out

Alan started running competitively in the seventh grade. As a freshman at Austintown Fitch High School, Alan ran an impressive 4:24 mile and progressively lowered his time to a 4:09 as a senior. Even with these impressive mile times Alan considered himself more of a two miler in high school. A fact that cannot be argued because Alan has recorded the fastest two mile time of any Ohio high school runner, posting a 8:44 at the 1978 Golden West National High School Track Meet. Even being tagged as a two miler, Alan was by no means slow and was able to run a 1:57 half-mile in high school.

Alan's state mile title came in his senior year when he ran a 4:13. The previous week at District he ran a 4:09 to win the mile heat.

Alan ran all four seasons of cross country at Austintown Fitch High School outside of Youngstown. After the cross country season he continued to run throughout the winter logging 55 to 60 miles a week. Alan would only take a few weeks off after the cross country season, starting to run again in early December. During the Christmas season college runners would be home for the holidays and Alan would train with them. He also attended several indoor meets during the winner.

Spring Training

During the spring track season Alan would run 45 to 50 miles a week. This included Sunday runs of 10 miles. The typical week for Alan during the spring season was running 8 miles on Monday on a somewhat hilly course averaging about 6:30 per mile. Tuesday was a dual-meet where he would typically run three or four distance events. Wednesday would be an easy eight mile recovery run. Thursday would again be 8 miles on the road running harder at a six minute mile pace. Friday would be an easy four or five miles before the meet on Saturday.

The surprising part of Alan's workout routine is that he almost never ran workouts on a track. Having a dual-meet every Tuesday served as the stand-in for a fast interval track workout. As the season progressed Alan would start running quarter mile events such as the mile relay and the open 440 in the Tuesday dual meets.

Alan did a lot of stretching after these practices, his high school coach believing that stretching was most beneficial after the muscles had warmed up. He did no weightlifting or calisthenics during his high school years. Cross training for high school runners was not common at the time Alan competed; however, he played basketball two or three times a week in the winter and did a lot of swimming and water skiing in the summer.

Tapering and Race Day

At the end of the season during the week of State, Alan would do a long slow run on Sunday. Monday and Tuesday he would do his regular 8 mile loop finishing up on the track and doing a few strides. Thursday and Friday would be an easy four or 5 miles. Alan's coach had him working hard up until the week of state. The week of Sectional and District would be hard effort weeks and only the week of state would be a lower effort.

Race day routine for Alan consisted of staying under the stands and avoiding the heat. Alan would jog for 15 minutes, 45 minutes before his race. Next would be some stretching, putting on his spikes, followed by a few strides. Eating on race day for Alan consisted of sandwiches and Gatorade. Alan was not a big fan of breakfast and usually did not have one on race day.

Junior year in high school Alan met the famous distance runner Alberto Salazar, forming a relationship that paid off for Alan with some free running shoes. Alan had the same shoe size as Alberto and would get leftovers and hand-me-downs from the Nike sponsored runner.

Ohio High School State Mile Champions

Alan Scharsu Stats and Traits and Habits

Started running at age.	12
Eating the night before a race.	Pasta
Eating the day of a race.	Sandwich and Gatorade
Running on Sundays.	Yes 10 miles
Running cross country.	Yes
Running after the cross country season.	Yes – 2 week break
Miles per week during the track season.	45 miles/week
Miles per week during the winter.	55 miles/week
Ran indoor track.	Yes – 2/3 meets
Ran weekday dual meets during track season.	Yes – one every Tues
Number of interval workouts during the week.	Dual Tuesday
Height	5'7"
Weight	115
Fastest mile was run at State.	Yes
Doubled up at State Meet.	Yes - 2 mile
Weight lifting.	No
Stretching	Basic - after
Calisthenics.	No
Tapering for week of state.	Yes
Eating before the gun.	Yes
Running twice a day	No
Cross training.	No
Fastest 800	NA
Fastest 400	NA
Training Method	Lydiard – Tempo Runs

John Zishka
Lancaster High School - 1979
"A lot of the running I did was fast running.
When it was time to run, I ran hard."

While the 1970s came in fast for Ohio high school milers, they left even faster. 1979 would see the fastest Ohio high school miler to date, John Zishka from Lancaster. During the summer of 1979, John ran a 4:03.8 mile, ranking him as the 19th fastest high school miler ever in the US to date.

Starting Out

John started running in seventh grade. Before high school John was active in basketball playing up until his freshman year at Lancaster High School.

In track as a freshman John ran just under a 4:30 mile. The next year as a sophomore he ran a 4:15 mile. Junior year saw John run a 4:08. John's fastest mile his senior year was not at state meet. He had run a faster time the week before state at District. The fastest mile of his high school career came in the summer of his senior year when he ran a 4:03.8 at the Golden Meet West.

John had different coaches in high school for cross country and track, and they both had different training philosophies. His cross country coach, Bob Reel, believed in an Arthur Lydriad-type of program that included a lot of long slow miles. Bob now coaches in Montana where his team recently won the high school state cross country championship.

John's track coach was a believer in intervals, more along the Igloi training method. John believes that the mileage base in the fall helped develop his strength for spring track.

Spring Training

A big change for John came during his junior year when he started to run year-round. This change allowed John to progressively do more mileage as he got older.

John competed in the indoor track season in January, February and part of March. During the winter, John would run approximately 50

33

miles a week. His senior year he had a few winter training weeks where he would log 60 to 70 miles a week. The winter season workouts consisted of long mileage peppered with indoor meets. There were no interval or speed workouts during the indoor season.

During the track season, John's workouts consisted of intervals and these alternated between long intervals one week to short intervals the next week. The longer intervals consisted of three quarters or half-mile repeats, a threshold type of workout, sometimes on the grass. The short interval workout the following week would consist of quarter-mile workouts. John would run 8 to 12 quarter miles at race pace or faster. The month of May consisted of faster shorter intervals. For John, the track intervals workouts started in March and lasted eight weeks.

John also did weightlifting in the winter and spring. This weightlifting was a supervised program for the runners and throwers on the track team. The training consisted of core workouts and upper body exercises with very little focus on lower body exercises. John's track coach emphasized stretching and John spent a lot of time on stretching. John stretched for approximately 15 minutes before 15 minutes after the workout.

Tapering and Race Day

John always made an effort to extend his peak past the state meet. All through high school he ran into the month of June in Junior Olympic and at age group meets. The week of District and State John backed his mileage down from 50 to 35 miles a week. During this taper, he would still run 8 or 9 miles on Sunday, but during the week his workouts became shorter, concentrating on fast short intervals repeats of 400m to 300m.

An example of one of these tapering workouts was running cut down 300m intervals where they would run five 300m as fast as they could with a 5 to 6 minute rest in between them, almost a complete recovery.

John's race day food intake consisted of fruits and breads. Race day routine consisted of walking the track and visualizing the race a couple hours before the gun. 60 minutes before the gun he would jog for 10 to 15 minute, do some light stretching 30 minutes before the gun, go for another light jog and then 15 minutes before the race do some accelerations to get the heart rate up. John was very regimented in his race day preparation and the night before he would have his race day equipment laid and out ready to go.

Ohio High School State Mile Champions

John Zishka Stats and Traits and Habits

Started running at age.	11
Eating the night before a race.	No Specific
Eating the day of a race.	Fruit
Running on Sundays.	Yes 9 miles
Running cross country.	Yes
Running after the cross country season.	Yes
Miles per week during the track season.	40 miles/week
Miles per week during the winter.	50 miles/week
Ran indoor track.	Yes
Ran weekday dual meets during track season.	Yes
Number of interval workouts during the week.	One
Height	5'8""
Weight	130
Fastest mile was run at State.	No
Doubled up at State Meet.	NA
Weight lifting.	Yes
Stretching	Basic - before
Calisthenics.	No
Tapering for week of state.	Yes
Eating before the gun.	Yes
Running twice a day	No
Cross training.	No
Fastest 800	NA
Fastest 400	NA
Training Method	Lydiard/CC – Igloi/Track

1980's

Cause I'm back on the track
and I'm beatin' the pack.
Nobody's gonna get me on the money lap.
Back In Black - AC/DC

Ohio High School State Mile Champions

Clark Haley
Lancaster High School - 1981

"I did not want to run the mile at state. I was gearing towards the half-mile, but they ran the 1600m so slow they just handed me the win."

Starting Out

Clark started running cross country his freshman year in high school. However, he did not run track until his junior year. Clark did not like running and even stated that he hated it. However, the combination of a persistent freshman cross country coach and his friends going out for the team pushed him onto the freshman cross country team. As a sophomore playing baseball Clark was beaned in the face causing him to look for another sport. He tried out for the golf team, but the golf coach pushed him towards track.

As a junior running track Clark did not race the 1600m as he focused more on the 800m and ran a 1:53.7 that year. After cross country season of Clark's senior year, he continued running with no break. For winter training Clark ran 6 to 8 miles a day seven days a week. This was the first winter that Clark trained through. Running during the winter consisted of mostly running the same 6 mile loop every day. Clark also ran a handful of indoor meets during the winter of his senior year.

Clark's senior year at state he doubled up in the 1600m and 800m. At state he was more focused on running and winning the 800m, and he had the fastest state meet qualifying time at 1:53.7. He ended up winning the state 1600m due to a very slow first three laps that let Clark sprint the last 300m of the bell lap and win with a 4:14. His 800m race had a different outcome.

You could say that at the state meet, Clark was in the right place at the right time for winning the 1600m, quickly followed by being in the wrong place at the wrong time. After winning the 1600m and crossing the finish line Clark sat down to remove his spikes and had the unfortunate fate of being near an OSU college student trainer with a large bucket of ice. Thinking that Clark was in heat exhaustion, the student trainer poured the bucket of ice water on him. This sent Clark into shock from which he could not recover and 45 minutes later, he started the 800m, but only jogged through the race and did not place.

Spring Training

During the track season Clark would average about 55 miles a week. Workouts consisted of a lot of ladder workouts of shorter distances and quarter mile workouts. He rarely ran any longer intervals such as mile repeats. At the beginning of the track season, workouts consisted of longer mileage for Clark, middle of the season consisted of interval workouts consisting of a lot of quarter mile and 200m repeat workouts. A standard workout would be a dozen quarter miles all run at a 60 to 65 second pace.

Although Clark's high school coach constantly sent him to the weight room, Clark did little, if any, weight lifting. Clark always stretched for 20 minutes before running and 50 sit ups after.

Tapering and Race Day

For tapering at the end of the season, Clark reduced the number of intervals by half and warm-ups would be at a slower pace. Workouts during the tapering period consisted of a dozen 100m or 200m intervals on the track.

Clark had no special diet or meal the night before a meet. Eating the day of the race consisted of two slices of jelly toast for breakfast. Clark liked to stay away from the simple sugar foods and to eat fructose based foods.

Race day routine consisted of running two miles, 60 minutes before the gun. This was followed by stretching and some hundred meter strides.

Ohio High School State Mile Champions

Clark Haley Stats and Traits and Habits

Started running at age.	17
Eating the night before a race.	No spec
Eating the day of a race.	Toast and jelly
Running on Sundays.	Yes 6 miles
Running cross country.	Yes
Running after the cross country season.	Yes – No break
Miles per week during the track season.	50 miles/week
Miles per week during the winter.	60 miles/week
Ran indoor track.	Yes – 2-3 meets
Ran weekday dual meets during track season.	Yes
Number of interval workouts during the week.	2/week
Height	6'0"
Weight	135
Fastest mile was run at State.	Yes 4:14
Doubled up at State Meet.	Yes
Weight lifting.	Yes
Stretching	Basic - before
Calisthenics.	Yes
Tapering for week of state.	Yes
Eating before the gun.	Yes
Running twice a day	Yes
Cross training.	Yes
Fastest 800	1:53
Fastest 400	51
Training Method	Igloi – short intervals

Rollie Hudson
Cleveland Heights High School – 1983, 1984

"On the back stretch of the last lap I was third or fourth and I remember a feeling of glee came over me because I knew I was going to win."

Starting Out

Rollie Hudson started running in seventh grade as a byproduct of training for wrestling. While most wrestlers universally disliked running laps around the gym or school, Rollie enjoyed it. That following spring he started running track with his friends.

Forbidden by his mother to play football, Rollie started running cross country his sophomore year at Cleveland Heights and continued his junior and senior years. Rollie placed 35th in the state cross country meet his junior year and fourth his senior year. This fourth-place finish his senior year was a disappointment coming off his 1600m state championship the previous spring.

Rollie's junior track season was his breakout year when he lowered his 1600m time from the 4:30s to sub 4:20s. He won state his junior year in the 1600m. The 1600m win was somewhat unexpected because he had to run against the heavily favored Bob Mauw. However, Bob sprained his ankle the week before state and was not a contender. Rollie had focused more on the 800m than the 1600m. He ran a 1:52 800m this senior year but he did not double at state, preferring to concentrate on the 1600m much to the consternation of his coach.

Rollie ran year round, frequently running in the evenings during the summer and winter. During the winter, he would run 6 to 8 miles per day averaging approximately 50 miles a week. Rollie would continue his daily running right after the cross country state meet. He frequently ran the same five-mile loop around his home in Cleveland Heights.

Rollie had an indoor schedule of meets in the winter for which he did some speed training. This was done in one of the hallways at Cleveland Heights High School. A large corridor 100m in length with a steel pole at both ends served as an indoor track. Meets were also held in the corridor. One of Rollie's big indoor wins was at the Knights of Columbus indoor invitational at the Coliseum his senior year.

41

Ohio High School State Mile Champions

Spring Training

Rollie frequently ran on Sundays during the track season. Mileage on these Sunday runs depended on how hard racing was the day before at the Saturday meet - three to five miles if Saturday was a hard meet, 8 miles if the Saturday meet was not as strenuous.

During the track season, Rollie typically logged 35 to 40 miles per week. This would be a mix of hard track interval workouts with a 6 to 7 mile road run. The typical week in the spring would be a distance run on Monday followed by a hard interval track workout or dual meet on Tuesday. Wednesday would be a moderate mileage recovery run. Thursday would be a workout on the track concentrating on fast turnover. Friday was usually a nonrunning travel day spent on a bus. One of the harder track interval workouts for Rollie was 6 to 8 x 400m repeats at 55 seconds with a one minute rest.

Rollie did weight training throughout the year. This consisted of short sessions with lighter weights. This weight training was done after the track workout. Rollie would religiously stretch before a hard track workout but conversely almost never stretch before long road runs. Rollie was also an accomplished high jumper who set his middle school record at 6'2" and jumped 6'4" his sophomore year.

Rollie considers his track season training the classic method, longer base miles at the beginning, followed by intervals midseason that got shorter and faster, finishing up with tapering/sharpening period at the end of the season.

Tapering and Race Day

To taper for the week of state, Rollie did no long road runs. Monday and Tuesday consisted of light speed workouts. Wednesday and Thursday contained a fast quarter mile workout.

Race day routine for Rollie consisted of jogging two miles, stretching, followed by some 30m sprints. Eating on race day for Rollie was a light breakfast three hours before the gun and little else.

Rollie's race strategy at state meet was to not take the lead but to run right behind the leaders. He would then let his kick win the race, which he would begin 300m from the finish.

Ohio High School State Mile Champions   *www.highschooldistancerunning.com*

Rollie Hudson Stats and Traits and Habits

Started running at age.	12
Eating the night before a race.	No spec
Eating the day of a race.	Bread and water
Running on Sundays.	Yes 3-8 miles
Running cross country.	Yes
Running after the cross country season.	Yes – 1 week off
Miles per week during the track season.	35 miles/week
Miles per week during the winter.	50 miles/week
Ran indoor track.	Yes
Ran weekday dual meets during track season.	Yes – one every week
Number of interval workouts during the week.	One
Height	6'2"
Weight	160
Fastest mile was run at State.	Yes
Doubled up at State Meet.	No
Weight lifting.	Yes
Stretching	Yes - before
Calisthenics.	Light
Tapering for week of state.	Yes
Eating before the gun.	Yes
Running twice a day	No
Cross training.	No
Fastest 800	1:52
Fastest 400	51
Training Method	Igloi – intervals

43

Ohio High School State Mile Champions

Scott Fry
Sandusky Perkins High School – 1984,1985

"I was a distance runner, I didn't have a lot of speed. The fastest I could run a quarter was 56 flat."

We have made an exception and gone down to Division II to detail Scott Fry's stellar high school running career. Scott is a standout for being the only Division II runner to have a faster state record time than the Division I event record. His 3200m state record of 8:46.7 is a full 10 seconds faster than John Zishka's Division I state record. Scott holds three state track records; the 800m, the 1600m, and the 3200m. His numerous track and cross-country state titles make him one of the most dominant distance runners in Ohio high school history.

Scott won the 1600m his senior year with a state record time of 4:08 which was also his fastest time of the year. Less than two hours after winning the 1600m, Scott ran an 8:49 3200m, a performance of doubling up at the State meet that has not been bettered to this day.

Starting Out

Scott started competitive running in the track season of his freshman year at Sandusky Perkins. The fall of his sophomore year he began running cross-country and he continued running after the season ended, only taking a week off after the state cross country meet. Scott ran throughout the winter logging approximately 90 miles a week which included a long run on Sunday. Scott ran quite a few indoor meets during the winter and competed a fair amount year-round. He logged 83 races his senior year in high school between cross-country, indoor and outdoor track.

Spring Training

During the track season, Scott's weekly mileage was 75 to 80 miles. His Sunday run was a 15 miler starting out at a 6:45 minute mile pace and working down to a six minute mile pace at the end. Scott did weight training on Nautilus machines two or three times a week during the winter. He discontinued this weight training during the track season. Scott did light stretching before workouts.

During early track season Scott ran a lot of Lydiard-type of workouts, including hills. This led to longer interval workouts, such as mile cutdowns, and as the season progressed the intervals became shorter and faster. The mile cutdown workouts consisted of four 1 mile repeats starting at a 4:50 pace and ending up at a 4:30 pace or better. Scott also ran half-mile and three quarters mile repeats. Ladder intervals of these same distances were a frequent workout during the midseason. There were usually six to eight intervals in a ladder workout that were run at a two-mile race pace. Towards the end of the track season intervals would shorten up to a quarter-mile. A typical workout would be 10 quarters at 60 seconds. Scott would typically have one meet during the week, the Saturday invitational and one interval workout. On the rest days he ran eight to 10 miles on the road. Scott also ran eight miles every week day morning in addition to his after school workouts.

Tapering and Race Day

The week of state Scott knocked his mileage back to 60 miles a week and did not include any long runs. Intervals during the week of state were short and fast. These would be sharpening workouts consisting of fast 600m or 300m repeats with a lot of rest.

For pre-race routine, Scott would run a two mile jog 20 minutes before the gun. He then put on his spikes and did six or seven strides. Scott was religious about not eating six hours before his race.

Ohio High School State Mile Champions

Scott Fry Stats and Traits and Habits

Started running at age.	13
Eating the night before a race.	No Spec
Eating the day of a race.	None
Running on Sundays.	Yes 15 miles
Running cross country.	Yes
Running after the cross country season.	Yes – No break
Miles per week during the track season.	75 miles/week
Miles per week during the winter.	90 miles/week
Ran indoor track.	Yes - 6 meets
Ran weekday dual meets during track season.	Yes – one every week
Number of interval workouts during the week.	Dual Tuesday
Height	5'6"
Weight	118
Fastest mile was run at State.	Yes
Doubled up at State Meet.	Yes 3200m
Weight lifting.	Winter only
Stretching	Basic - before
Calisthenics.	No
Tapering for week of state.	Yes
Eating before the gun.	No
Running twice a day	Yes
Cross training.	No
Fastest 800	NA
Fastest 400	56
Training Method	Lydiard & spring intervals

Mark Groghan
Franklin Furnace Green High School - 1986
"I was an old-school runner.
If I wanted to get better running, I ran more."

As a three time steeplechase Olympian and fourth in the 1994 World Championships, Mark can show us something about winning the state mile and doing it without having 400m speed.

Starting Out

Mark started running in seventh-grade and ran a 5:27 mile that season. As an eighth grader, Mark ran 5:02. He says that he then somewhat stalled out lowering his times during his freshman, sophomore and junior years in high school. He broke five minutes as a freshman, a standout performance, but by his junior year had run only a 4:36.

Mark considered himself more of a cross country and strength runner, than a miler. He qualified for state in cross country all four years in high school but only qualified for the state track meet his senior year. His senior year, Mark won the 1600m at State with a 4:10. Running the mile at state was almost an afterthought. Mark's real goal was to win the 3200m, but he ran the 1600m to score points for his team, which ended up winning state that year. His qualifying state time for the 3200m was 10 seconds faster than anyone else. However, his 1600m state qualifying time was approximately fifth best. At the state meet, Mark won in the mile with a personal best of 4:10 and came back to win the 3200m in 9:19.

After Mark's freshman cross country season and through his junior year he did not run in the winter, instead playing basketball. Mark was not all that crazy about running around in circles on a track during the spring and he did not have a lot of motivation to run in the snow during the winter for the track season. Mark won state cross country as a junior. However, as a senior he did not repeat this victory, leaving a bad taste in his mouth and motivating him do train through the winter and redeem himself the next spring.

That winter, Mark started training January 1 and ran consistently everyday through the entire winter - not high mileage, just 3 miles every morning before school. This was supplemented with afternoon runs of 6 miles approximately every other day, averaging approximately 30 to 35 miles a week. Mark also ran indoor meets

Ohio High School State Mile Champions

during the winter of his senior year. At one indoor meet, Mark ran a 9:36 minute two mile, faster than he had ever run a two mile on an outdoor track.

Spring Training

During the track season Mark ran on Sundays logging 8 to 12 miles. In the early part of the track season, Mark would go to Firestone Park in Akron once a week and do a hill work out.

In the spring, Mark ran a lot of midweek meets, sometimes running three meets a week. That did not leave a lot of time for workouts. When Mark wasn't racing he was doing recovery runs. Mark would typically run three events in these meets and his high school coaches concentrated on putting Mark in the 800m as frequently as possible. There was no standard week to week workout routine for Mark and he did not run workouts on the track until the end of the season during the District and Regional meet weeks. These end-of-season practices consisted of quarter-mile workouts where his teammates would alternate running intervals with him. These intervals were typically 8 x 400m with 60 seconds rest, at low 60s second pace.

Tapering and Race Day

Tapering at the end of the season consisted of cutting back the mileage the week of state and doing easy 5 mile road runs and no heavy track workouts.

Mark's race day routine was running two miles 60 minutes before the race followed by some basic stretching and strides. Mark would have a standard pancakes or eggs breakfast four hours before the race.

Mark's race strategy was to run in the lead, dictate a fast pace and remove the finishing kick from the faster runners. He would end with a controlled kick 600m out from the finish.

Mark Groghan Stats and Traits and Habits

Started running at age.	12
Eating the night before a race.	No Spec
Eating the day of a race.	Pancakes - eggs
Running on Sundays.	Yes 8-12 miles
Running cross country.	Yes
Running after the cross country season.	Yes – One month
Miles per week during the track season.	40 miles/week
Miles per week during the winter.	35 miles/week
Ran indoor track.	Yes – One Meet
Ran weekday dual meets during track season.	Yes – one every week
Number of interval workouts during the week.	One/week
Height	5'8"
Weight	125
Fastest mile was run at State.	Yes
Doubled up at State Meet.	Yes - 3200
Weight lifting.	No
Stretching	Basic - before
Calisthenics.	No
Tapering for week of state.	Yes
Eating before the gun.	Yes
Running twice a day	Yes - winter
Cross training.	No
Fastest 800	1:57
Fastest 400	58
Training Method	Racing and Igloi

Ohio High School State Mile Champions

Bob Kennedy
Westerville North High School – 1987, 1988
"I never ran to do mileage, I always ran for a purpose."

Bob holds the State of Ohio high school record for the 1600m, is a four time NCAA champion, a two time Olympian and set two American track records.

Starting Out

Bob started competitive running in the seventh grade at Walnut Springs middle school in Westerville, Ohio. His first cross country season was freshman year in high school.

At state meet junior year Bob doubled up in the 1600m and the 3200m. Senior year he did not double up, only running and winning the 1600m. He did not double his senior year because his team was not in contention to win state and he did not have a compelling reason to run a second race for more points. Bob's state winning 1600m time his junior and senior years were the fastest times of the season for him. Bob's 4:05 time for state his senior year is currently the Ohio high school 1600m state record.

Bob ran cross country all four years in high school. After cross country he would take two to four weeks off before starting to train for the track season. Bob's cross country season ended after national meets in early December. He typically logged 30 miles per week in the winter. This consisted of what Bob calls a lot of quality running such as fartlek workouts and running pickups from telephone pole to telephone pole. Bob did not train on the track during the winter. He did structured weight training during the winter till the start of track season in March. This weight training was twice a week under a coach's supervision and mostly consisted of core body workouts.

Bob ran some casual indoor meets during the winter at Otterbein College and also some high profile indoor meets such as the Millrose games and the Sunkist games in LA.

Spring Training

Bob professes that he was never a big mileage runner in high school. During the track season he never ran more than 25 to 30 miles a week. As Bob comments, it was all quality. However, Bob mentions that if he had to do it all over again he would have liked to have run 40 to 50 miles a week. He rarely ran on Sundays during the track season and a long run for him would be 6 miles.

Bob did not have any rituals for calisthenics or stretching. Stretching consisted of the standard 15 minutes before the workout. Warmup consisted of a half-mile around the track before a workout.

Bob's practice schedule for the track season consisted of the classic longer intervals at the beginning of the season, leading into shorter intervals in a late-season, followed by a tapering period for peaking. During the track season Bob ran a dual meet every week and sometimes two dual meets a week. Bob would treat these dual meets as workouts sometimes running four races per meet. Bob would treat each race in these dual meets as a specific workout. For example, when he ran the mile, each lap would have a specific target pace. He would run the first lap in 69 seconds, the next two laps in 60 seconds and the fourth lap in 69 seconds. If there was not a second dual meet during the week, Bob would do a track workout on Thursday. Continuous relays were a favorite workout. This consisted of three runners on the team each running 200m legs and handing the baton off to the next runner.

Tapering and Race Day

Tapering for state week consisted of reducing the volume of intervals. A typical workout for the week of state would consist of five quarter mile repeats. Rest periods during these quarter miles were also extended. The tapering period consisted of two weeks before state meet. Bob also determined how much he would reduce workouts for tapering two weeks before state depending on how hard the competition was for that regional meet. If it was a slower field, he would not taper as much.

Race day consisted of a pancake breakfast four hours before the race. No additional foods before the gun, no power bars or drinks. Warming up before the race consisted of jogging 15 to 20 minutes 60 minutes before the race. Bob's race tactic for the state 1600m of his senior year was to run an exact pace of 61 second 400m laps, thinking that if he ran a 4:04 he would win the race.

Ohio High School State Mile Champions

Bob Kennedy Stats and Traits and Habits

Started running at age.	13
Eating the night before a race.	No Specific Meal
Eating the day of a race.	Pancakes
Running on Sundays.	Rarely- 6 miles
Running cross country.	Yes
Running after the cross country season.	Yes – 2 months
Miles per week during the track season.	25 miles/week
Miles per week during the winter.	30 miles/week
Ran indoor track.	Yes - 2 meets
Ran weekday dual meets during track season.	Yes – one every week
Number of interval workouts during the week.	One
Height	6'0"
Weight	150
Fastest mile was run at State.	Yes
Doubled up at State Meet.	Yes
Weight lifting.	Yes Winter only
Stretching	Basic - before
Calisthenics.	No
Tapering for week of state.	Yes
Eating before the gun.	Yes
Running twice a day	No
Cross training.	No
Fastest 800	1:52
Fastest 400	50
Training Method	Iglod & Tempo Runs

1990's

Boys and things that come by the dozen
That ain't nothin but drugstore lovin
Hey little thing let me light your candle
cause mama I'm sure hard to handle, now.
Hard to Handle – Black Crows

Ohio High School State Mile Champions

Darrell Hughes
Galloway Westland High School - 1990, 1991
"At state junior and senior year I doubled in the 1600m and 800m and won them all."

Starting Out

A two-time winner from Galloway Westland High School, Darrell was king of the 1600m and 800m for two years, doubling up in these events in 1990 and 1991 and winning both events both years. His 1600m times were 4:10 and under and his 800m times were 1:52 and lower. After the state meet Darrell's senior year, he ran in the Keebler National with a 4:08 mile and posted a 3:47 1500m at the TAC nationals.

Darrell ran cross country all four years in high school and took approximately two weeks off after the cross country season before he started his winter training. In December, he would run every other day and then, starting in January, would run six days a week. The average miles per week during the winter would be 40. Every Monday during the winter he would go to the French Fieldhouse at Ohio State University to run an interval workout. These indoor track workouts were not fast intervals, more along the lines of keeping the heart rate up for a specific time. Saturdays during the winter were long runs of 10 to 12 miles. Darrell only competed in one indoor track meet.

Darrell did weight lifting during the winter and early track season. This consisted mostly of upper body exercises and were on the lighter side.

Spring Training

During the track season Darrell averaged approximately 35 miles a week. He ran long runs of 10 to 14 miles on Sunday during the track season. Every Sunday run was on a different course.

Dual meets were once a week. Typical track workout schedule for the week was an easy four or five miles on Monday. He ran a dual meet on Tuesday but did not run the 1600m or 800m and instead ran in the 200m and 400m events. Wednesday would be a hard interval workout. Thursday sometimes would be an off day and Friday would be an easy three or 4 miles followed by some 200m strides. Darrell's distance runs were typically run at a seven minute mile pace.

54

Wednesday workouts were always different. Some typical Wednesday workouts were 1000m, 800m or 500m repeats. One workout was running four sets of 4 x 300m repeats. Another workout was a ladder of 4 x 150m, 2 x 600m, followed by 4 x 200m intervals.

Tapering and Race Day

The week of state meet, Darrell ran 90 minutes on Sunday, followed by five miles on Monday. Tuesday was 50 minutes of running on the grass. Wednesday Darrell did four sets of 150m with a 50m rest between. This was followed by a 600m, 400m, 200m, 100m ladder that was repeated twice. Thursday was off, and Friday was 4 miles followed by some 150m strides. Darrell tried to keep the mileage up during this taper for state because he ran national meets in the month of June and July.

60 to 90 minutes before the race Darrell would do 15 minutes of jogging followed by stretching. This was followed by some 50m strides. Warmups were never strenuous; Darrell always tried to save energy for the race.

Race day diet consisted of eating a bowl of cereal in the morning followed by drinking one or two cans of Exceed power drink. Darrell liked this power drink because it was quickly digestible. He would not eat or drink between the 1600m and 800m races. Eating the night before consisted of going out with the team for a pasta dinner.

Ohio High School State Mile Champions

Darell Hughs Stats and Traits and Habits

Started running at age.	12
Eating the night before a race.	Pasta
Eating the day of a race.	Cereal and protein drink
Running on Sundays.	Yes 10 miles
Running cross country.	Yes
Running after the cross country season.	Yes – 45 day break
Miles per week during the track season.	35 miles/week
Miles per week during the winter.	40 miles/week
Ran indoor track.	Yes - 1 meet
Ran weekday dual meets during track season.	Yes
Number of interval workouts during the week.	One Wednesday
Height	6'1"
Weight	160
Fastest mile was run at State.	Yes
Doubled up at State Meet.	Yes
Weight lifting.	Yes
Stretching	Basic - before
Calisthenics.	No
Tapering for week of state.	Yes
Eating before the gun.	Yes
Running twice a day	No
Cross training.	No
Fastest 800	1:52
Fastest 400	50
Training Method	Igloi – intervals

Ohio High School State Mile Champions   www.highschooldistancerunning.com

Mason Ward
Cincinnati Colerain High School – 1994,1995

"Senior year at state I was defending champion. No one wanted to challenge me and we came through a half-mile in 2:12. I said the heck with this and ran the next half-mile in 1:57."

Mason is a two time state champion and so good that they named a race after him. As of the publishing of the first edition, Mason was serving in Afghanistan with the US Army.

Starting Out

Mason started running in seventh grade. He ran cross country all four years in high school but had more success running track, becoming a standout in the 1600m. Mason ran a 4:21 1600m as a freshman and progressively lowered his 1600m time every year, running a 4:07 as a senior.

Mason won the 1600m state title his junior and senior year. His junior year his state mile time was the fastest of the season. His senior year his state winning 1600m time was not his quickest of the season. Mason did not double up at the state meet, although he frequently ran the 800m and the 3200m races at the District and Regional meets.

After cross country season Mason trained throughout the winter and competed in indoor track which included the Milrose games. Mason's senior year he took a month off after cross country to recover from a back injury. During the winter indoor season, training consisted of strength runs, such as to mile or three-mile repeats. Mason did no interval training or tapering during the indoor season. At indoor meets, Mason ran the 800m more often than the 1600m. During the winter months Mason ran 50 miles a week in January and this would increase to 60 to 65 miles a week in February and March.

Spring Training

Mason was religious about running every Sunday, logging 10 to 12 miles on these runs. He also did weight training in the winter and spring, lifting three times a week on Sunday, Tuesday and Thursday. This weight training varied from season to season but mostly consisted of upper body workouts. Mason stretched both before and after his workouts but did no calisthenics during the track season. Post workout warm down routines consisted of running 3 to 6 x 100m strides.

57

Ohio High School State Mile Champions

During the track season Mason ran few, if any, dual meets during the week. Racing was only on Saturdays and only in big invitationals. Also unique was that Mason only ran in one 1600m race his senior year before the state tournament meets, that was the Penn relays. Instead of running the 1600m on Saturdays, Mason would run the 400m and 800m with the purpose of building speed.

Interval speed training did not start until the end of March/early April. The typical weekly workout schedule for Mason consisted of two speed workouts. Midseason meets were worked through by running a hard 6 or 7 miles on Friday. Speed workouts consisted of a lot of 800m, 400m and 300m intervals. The start of the track season intervals would be longer, consisting of 1000m and 800m intervals. At the end of the season intervals became very fast. 400m repeats were run at 58 seconds and 200m were run in 26 seconds.

Tapering and Race Day

Tapering for state meet consisted of knocking down mileage to 35 miles the week of state and running 200m repeats.

Diet did not factor too much into Mason's training. Typically, dinner the night before a meet was either pasta or pizza. Eating race day consisted of cereal for breakfast followed by power bars or sandwiches. His prerace routine consisted of running a mile and a half 60 minutes before the gun, followed by stretching 40 minutes before the gun with some strides 20 minutes before the gun.

Mason Ward Stats and Traits and Habits

Started running at age.	12
Eating the night before a race.	Pasta/Pizza
Eating the day of a race.	Cereal
Running on Sundays.	Yes 10 miles
Running cross country.	Yes
Running after the cross country season.	Yes – 30 day break
Miles per week during the track season.	60 miles/week
Miles per week during the winter.	55 miles/week
Ran indoor track.	Yes - 5 meets
Ran weekday dual meets during track season.	Few
Number of interval workouts during the week.	Two
Height	6'0"
Weight	155
Fastest mile was run at State.	Yes
Doubled up at State Meet.	No
Weight lifting.	Yes
Stretching	Basic - before
Calisthenics.	No
Tapering for week of state.	Yes
Eating before the gun.	Yes
Running twice a day	No
Cross training.	No
Fastest 800	1:56
Fastest 400	51
Training Method	Igloi & Tempo Runs

Ohio High School State Mile Champions

2000's

I'm hot coz I'm fly
You ain't coz you're not
This is why, this is why
This is why I'm hot.
Mims - This Is Why I'm Hot

Ohio High School State Mile Champions

Jeff See
Middletown High School – 2003, 2004, 2005
"As a sophomore I had a really good year and ran a 4:06."

Some really great runners come from families where the older brothers and/or sisters hand down the sport. The only three time state 1600m champion, Jeff See, qualifies as one of these runners.

Starting Out

Jeff started competitive running in the seventh grade. At that time he also played basketball and soccer. Jeff got into cross country because he had a brother who was four years older and who had run cross-country. By the time Jeff was a freshman, he ran a 4:15 1600m and placed second at state. As a sophomore, he ran a 4:06 and won the state 1600m. An illness slowed Jeff down his junior year but he still won the state 1600m that year. As a senior, he lowered his 1600m time to 4:03. Jeff won state in the 1600m as sophomore, junior and senior. His senior year he also doubled up and won the 800m in 1:51.2.

Jeff ran cross country all four years in high school. After the cross country season the months of November and December were light training months. Jeff took the month of November off and then in December would run 20 to 30 minutes a day. Jeff also played basketball during this time. In January, he would start picking up the pace and run harder. Jeff's junior and senior years he ran approximately 50 miles a week during January and February, then moved up to 60 miles a week throughout the rest of the track season. Jeff would not get on the track for workouts until early March. He never ran indoor track with the exception of a national meet, the Nike invitational his freshman year, where he set a 1600m indoor national record.

Jeff did weight training only during the cross country season and this consisted of light repetition weights. Jeff did this up until his junior year when he started his own calisthenics routine consisting mostly of core body workouts.

Spring Training

During the track season, Jeff ran approximately 10 miles every Sunday and this would be an easy work out. Jeff would start these 10 miles

62

runs around a 7 or 7:15 minute miles pace and by the end of the run work down to a 6:30-6:15 minute mile pace.

January and February running consisted of tempo workouts and mileage runs; never any track workouts. March and April workouts would move to the track where Jeff would run 1000m and 800m repeats. Middle of the season, track workouts consisted of race pace workouts such as ladders. Shorter intervals such as 400m and 200m repeats were not run until the last month of the track season in late April and May.

During the track season, Jeff rarely participated in dual meets during the week, and these few dual meets were only in the early-season. Later in the season, the sprinters would go to dual meets but the distance runners, including Jeff, would not, preferring to do workouts instead. Wednesday was the hard interval day for Jeff and most of the work week was pointed towards this hard effort day. Wednesday was the only day spent on the track, all other workouts were on the road. Monday was threshold running, Tuesday and Thursday were recovery days running on the roads, and Friday before a meet was a very light day on the roads. During the week the quality days were the Monday threshold run, the Wednesday track interval workout, the Saturday race and the Sunday tempo run.

Tapering and Race Day

Tapering would begin for the District meet, three weeks before the state meet. Mileage would never go under 35 miles a week during this time. The week before District, tapering would consist of 200m intervals on Monday, and 400m intervals on Wednesday. The other three days were light on the road. This weekly routine was repeated for the next two weeks.

For tapering and peaking, Jeff would cut out the Monday threshold run and run 200m repeats. Wednesday interval workouts would turn into race day simulation where he would run 4 x 400m repeats. Jeff's workouts and schedule were designed by Dave Fultz, the assistant track coach at Middletown.

Jeff's diet during his track season was staying away from acidic food such as citric fruits that gave him some digestive troubles. Poultry, pasta and potatoes were the staple during this time. Race day diet did not consist of any structured plan. Jeff would eat breakfast four hours before his race. Anything after breakfast or before the gun would only consist of a bagel or something very light.

Race day routine consisted of getting to the meet two hours before the race, 15 minutes of jogging 30 minutes before the race, running some long strides, then putting on his spikes 15 minutes before the gun and running some more strides. Jeff would continuously warmup for the 30 minutes before the gun.

Race day strategy for Jeff was knowing who he ran against, keying off these competitors, staying near them and always being close enough to win the race. Jeff never went into a race trying to run a set pace and he would not run in the lead but would always be close enough to apply pressure to the lead runner and influence the race.

Jeff See Stats and Traits and Habits

Started running at age.	13
Eating the night before a race.	Pasta, Chicken
Eating the day of a race.	Standard Breakfast
Running on Sundays.	Yes 10 miles
Running cross country.	Yes
Running after the cross country season.	Yes – 3 week break
Miles per week during the track season.	50 miles/week
Miles per week during the winter.	50 miles/week
Ran indoor track.	Yes
Ran weekday dual meets during track season.	No
Number of interval workouts during the week.	One Wednesday
Height	6'0"
Weight	150
Fastest mile was run at State.	Yes
Doubled up at State Meet.	Yes
Weight lifting.	Yes – Fall only
Stretching	Yes
Calisthenics.	Yes
Tapering for week of state.	Yes
Eating before the gun.	Yes
Running twice a day	No
Cross training.	No
Fastest 800	1:52
Fastest 400	48
Training Method	Igloi & tempo runs

65

Ohio High School State Mile Champions

Jake Edwards
Delaware Hayes High School - 2007

"My senior year I did something completely different. I found a method and followed it."

Starting Out

Jake started running cross country in seventh grade and started running track in ninth grade.

Jake captured the 2007 1600m title with a time of 4:09.9 which was his fastest time of the year. In the following weeks, he ran national meets where he lowered this time. Jake ran a 4:07 1600m at the Midwest meet of champions and the following week, at Nike Nationals, he ran a 4:08 mile.

Jake ran cross country in high school. However, training for cross country was not always what Jake called strenuous. There would be periods in the fall season where Jake would run only 25 miles a week and Jake never ran on Sundays in the fall. This was mostly due to practicing as a team and allowing more moderate runners to stay with the pack.

Jake's senior year he trained differently from his past track seasons. Starting in February, he began to run 55 to 60 miles a week. Jake had never run this high mileage during the winter. During this winter season, Jake ran some indoor meets. The training for these indoor meets came from the Jack Daniels book of training. This consisted of six weeks of base mileage, running 50 to 60 miles a week, followed by running 200m and 400m interval workouts and also 1000m interval workouts. He ran these workouts twice a week on an indoor track. These intervals were run at mile race pace and no faster. 200m repeats were run at 31 seconds. This practice produced a 4:18 at the indoor state meet. This race was run at a 300m indoor track in Akron and was a PR for Jake. It was also during the winter training that Jake started to run 13 miles on Sundays from February to late May.

Spring Training

Spring practice started with running longer intervals. For an early season workout, Jake ran a 800m, followed by a 1000m, followed by a mile and then cut back down. These were run at 70 second quarter mile pace. Midseason, these intervals shortened up. Jake would run a

66

400m and 200m workout. This consisted of sets of four repeats for each distance run at a faster 60 second quarter mile pace. Jake ran two interval workouts a week; one would be a longer threshold workout running 1000m repeats and the other workout would be a shorter speed interval workout. He always finished his workouts doing fast 200m repeats. Jake would run a workout of 10 quarter miles at a 60 second pace with a recovery period of one or two minutes. These intervals were run on a track.

Tapering and Race Day

Jake cut his Sunday runs down from 13 miles to 10 or 8 miles a week before state. Starting with the league meet, which was three weeks before state, Jake would not run on Fridays. Jake only ran a total of 40 miles the week of the league meet. This mileage stayed the same for the next two weeks where Jake doubled up at the District and Regional meets.

The week of state Jake ran 35 to 40 miles. Intervals the week of state consisted of only 200m repeats where Jake would run a half dozen intervals at 28 seconds. The last 200m would be run all out at 24 seconds.

Dinner the night before a race would consist of a whole wheat pasta meal. Race day Jake would have an egg and toast breakfast. Jake would also eat a container of apple sauce and a granola bar 90 minutes before the race. Jake would get to the meet two hours before the gun and preferred to stay out of the sun. 60 minutes before the race he would go for a 15 minute run, followed by some strides and stretching 30 minutes before the race started.

Jake did no weightlifting or rigorous calisthenics. He did a small amount of stretching before and/or after practices. Jake did no crosstraining or other sports, preferring to focus on running.

Ohio High School State Mile Champions

Jake Edwards Stats and Traits and Habits

Started running at age.	13
Eating the night before a race.	Pasta
Eating the day of a race.	Toast, eggs, apple
Running on Sundays.	Yes 12 miles
Running cross country.	Yes
Running after the cross country season.	Yes – 45 day break
Miles per week during the track season.	50 miles/week
Miles per week during the winter.	55 miles/week
Ran indoor track.	Yes
Ran weekday dual meets during track season.	Few
Number of interval workouts during the week.	Two
Height	5'11"
Weight	145
Fastest mile was run at State.	Yes
Doubled up at State Meet.	No
Weight lifting.	No
Stretching	No
Calisthenics.	No
Tapering for week of state.	Yes
Running twice a day	No
Cross training.	No
Fastest 800	NA
Fastest 400	NA
Training Method	Igloi

Danny Neff
Vandalia Butler High School – 2008, 09
"I never liked distance or tempo road runs, get me on the track and let's do some 400's."

Danny comes from a family of great high school athletes, both his grandfather and his father were standouts at Chaminade High School in Dayton Ohio. His father, Donald Neff, was on the 1970 high school baseball state championship team. Danny was headed for a high school sports career in baseball until a knee injury sidelined him. Looking for something to do in the spring, and at the encouragement of his uncle, Danny picked up track his freshman year and without a lot of training ran a 2:00 800m.

Starting Out

Danny won the State 1600m his junior and senior years, running a 4:15.9 his junior year and a 4:10.6 is senior year at Vandalia Butler high school. He also doubled his junior and senior year by running the 800m at state. His senior year he won both the 1600m and the 800m. Danny's fastest times senior year were a 4:08 1600m and a 1:50 800m.

Danny did not run cross country his freshman year and was not too serious about training his freshman year of track. Frequently, when told to go run distance, he would end up running over to the basketball courts for a game of pick up. His sophomore year he ran cross country, although he did not put much effort into this endeavor. The spring of his sophomore year Danny's high school coach, Andy White, persuaded Danny to work harder and this hard work produced a 4:20 1600m. This performance encouraged Danny to become serious about distance running.

Starting in his junior year during the cross-country season, Danny gave up his pickup basketball games and started logging 50 miles per week. A successful junior cross-country season led to a winter training program where Danny continued to run daily. Danny ran throughout the winter both his junior and senior year. He started in mid December running 35 miles a week, increased to 40 miles a week in January and increased to 45 miles a week in February. He ran only two indoor meets each season and he ran only hill workouts for interval/speed training. His ran his fastest indoor 1600m time his senior year, clocking a 4:12.

69

Ohio High School State Mile Champions

Spring Training

Danny's junior track season started in March with longer track intervals that ranged from 1200m to 400m intervals. In April, the intervals were reduced down to 400m - 200m repeats on the track. The bulk of Danny's intervals consisted of 8 x 400m workouts. These quarter-mile workouts were run at 60 second intervals with a one minute rest. In May, the quarter-mile workouts consisted of 8 x 400m run at 57 seconds with a three minute rest. Danny ran two intervals a week throughout the season. These intervals were on Tuesday and Thursday. At the beginning of the season, he ran one or two dual meets. As the season progressed, he stopped running dual meets, focusing on the workouts during the week. Danny made sure to run at least 55 miles every week during the season and his Sunday run was whatever distance was needed to reach his required 55 miles a week.

Besides running, Danny stretched lightly for 15 minutes at the beginning of each workout. He did no calisthenics, weightlifting or crosstraining.

Tapering and Race Day

Danny's tapering began three weeks before the state meet. For the district meet, Danny continued to run hard interval workouts consisting of a ladder workout of a 1200m, 800m, and 400m run hard. His weekly distance was reduced to 40 miles a week. Regional week Danny reduced his mileage to 35 miles a week and only ran one hard work out on Tuesday. His Thursday workout for that week consisted of 8 by 200m at an easy pace. By state week, Danny's mileage was down to 25 miles a week. For his Tuesday workout of state week, he ran 4 x 400m at 54 seconds and on Thursday he ran 4 x 200m at 30 seconds.

For race day, Danny warmed up 50 minutes before his race by running two miles. He would typically lie down and try to nap, staying calm and drinking water. 15 minutes before his race he would run some stride outs. For fuel, Danny would have a peanut butter and jelly sandwich three hours before his race. Food the night before was typically pizza.

Danny Neff Stats and Traits and Habits

Started running at age.	14
Eating the night before a race.	Pizza
Eating the day of a race.	Peanut Butter and Jelly
Running on Sundays.	Yes 5-10 miles
Running cross country.	Yes
Running after the cross country season.	Yes – 30 day break
Miles per week during the track season.	55 miles/week
Miles per week during the winter.	55 miles/week
Ran indoor track.	Yes
Ran weekday dual meets during track season.	Very Few
Number of interval workouts during the week.	Two
Height	6'0"
Weight	150
Fastest mile was run at State.	Yes
Doubled up at State Meet.	Yes
Weight lifting.	No
Stretching	A Little
Calisthenics.	No
Tapering for week of state.	Yes
Running twice a day	No
Cross training.	No
Fastest 800	1:51
Fastest 400	50.05
Training Method	Igloi

Training Methods

Many of our runners brought up three different training philosophies - Arthur Lydiard, Mihaly Igloi and Bob Schul. Now is a good time for a little schooling and background in the sport.

Auther Lydiard

Arthur Lydiard was a New Zealand distance running coach whose two most famous athletes, Peter Schnell and Lasse Viren, proved the effectiveness of his training method of base training and peaking. Lydiard's method consisted of a rest period following the end of a running season, then starting with base training that consisted of Long Slowed Distance (LSD), then doing hill training, and ending with a sharpening period. The base training period of LSD required over 100 miles a week.

Lasse Viren from Finland took Lanier's training to the extreme by extending the base training over a four-year Olympics cycle. During the years before the 1972 and 1976 Olympics, Viren competed very little, and when he did race he was usually beaten. However, when he sharpened and tapered once every four years immediately before the Olympics, he was unbeatable, winning both the 5000m in the 10,000m in both the 1972 and 1976 Olympics. He won his gold medals against other runners who had beaten him routinely throughout the previous seasons. When Viren peaked for the Olympics he was untouchable.

The three runners in this book that seem to follow Lanier's training method are Bill Beatty, Allen Scharsu, and Scott Fry.

Mihaly Igloi

Mihaly Igloi was a tyrant of a track coach who fled to the United States during the 1956 Hungarian revolution and coached some of the world's leading middle-distance runners. Igloi successively coached the Santa Monica Track Association and the Los Angeles Track Club. His runners broke 49 World and 45 American records.

Igloi coached American Bob Schul to the 1964 Olympic gold medal in the 5000 meters. He also coached such world-class milers as Sandor Iharos in Hungary and Laszlo Tabori and the cigarette-smoking Istvan

Rozsavolgyi in Hungary and the United States. He also coached such outstanding American milers as Jim Beatty and Dyrol Burleson.

Mihaly Igloi, who built his training system on interval training, based the intensity of the interval on the following descriptors of the progressive gradations leading up to race effort:
• easy—used for recovery
• medium easy—moderate effort
• medium—a little harder, but still conversational
• swing—fast, but still controlled
• fast—just as the name implies
• race—highest effort.

Most runners interviewed in this book followed Igloi's training methods.

Bob Schul

Bob Schul, from West Milton, Ohio, was the last American to win an Olympic gold-medal in the 5000m. After winning the gold-medal in 1964, Bob took up residence in the Dayton, Ohio area and by the mid-seventies was a continuous influence on many southwestern Ohio high school track and cross country runners. Bob's coaching and workouts were held at different tracks throughout the Dayton area and were always open to all comers.

Bob had a unique philosophy of training that benefited many athletes from high school runners to Olympic competitors. Bob's training was an Igloi type of interval base. Year-round workouts consisted of interval sets usually on the track. These workouts were run three times a week and lasted from two to three hours. Bob believes that the key to top performance is to keep the heart rate up for an extended period of time. This was done by running groups of intervals in one practice. A typical practice consisted of running 10 sets of 100m, followed by a half-mile jog. Next would be a six pack of quarter miles, again followed by a half mile jog. Another short distance interval was then run, typically 200m repeats, again followed by the half-mile jog. Finally, a longer set of intervals, anywhere from 300m to 600m. was run. In total, 5 to 6 sets of intervals were run during a practice.

Bob was never a big believer in road miles and stated that during the season of his Olympic gold-medal performance he ran approximately 35 miles a week. Teammates at Miami University would comment on Bob's practice of going underneath the football stadium and running constant repetitions of hundred meters strides. Bob also believes that

73

Ohio High School State Mile Champions

athletes can have a continuous cycle of race improvement and that cyclical seasonal routines of hard work, tapering, peaking and falling off are not mandatory.

Conclusions

"The bigger the base the higher the peak."
Dennis Bayham (NCAA Division I All American Steeplechaser)

The four things you need to win the state 1600m race are blind courage, unshakable faith, physical ability and the correct training program. I cannot help you with the first three. We can, through observation and analysis of how other champions trained, uncover the fourth one.

So we ask ourselves, after reading the interviews from these 17 state champions that collectively won over 20 titles in the last 40 years, what training and other factors did they all have in common that led to their running success? In other words, bottom-line, what does it take to run a 4:11 and win the state Division I 1600m and what factors are unimportant?

What's Not Important
Let's start with what I think is the easier category, what's not important. This list of what's not important are so termed because some runners included certain factors in their training while other runners did not. Also, there seems to be no clear trend on whether the runners that incorporated certain training factors ran any quicker than the runners that did not include them in their training. Let's look at them individually.

Weight Training
This category is evenly split with 50% of our runners doing some type of weight training and 50% of our runners doing no weight training. We can find no correlation demonstrating that weight training runners performed better than the runners that did no weight training. We can also lump calisthenics into this category. 75% of our runners did no calisthenics. We can sum up weight training as, if it makes you feel good do it, but it will not help us achieve our 4:11.

Not Running Weekday Dual Meets
Only three out of our 16 runners stated that they did not run dual meets, leaving the majority of our runners in the category of running one dual meet a week, most typically on Tuesday. These numbers end the argument of whether dual meets are bad for peak performance and disrupt the training schedule. While we are tempted to move the dual meet criteria from the "not important list" to the "what is important list" we did not do so because not every of our runners ran dual meets.

75

Ohio High School State Mile Champions

What we do note as being important from running dual meets is the fact that our runners who participated in one meet during the week treated them as a workout. Running several events from the 200m up, our runners used these Tuesday dual meets as an interval workout. The perfect example of this weekday dual meets as a workout is Alan Scharsu who held the national two mile record and never ran a workout on a track during the season. Instead, he ran a dual meet every Tuesday and used this meet as a substitute for working out on a track.. So our conclusion with dual meets is; are they necessary, no, can they can do harm, no, are they endorsed by the majority of our runners, yes.

Indoor Winter Racing
55 percent of our runners ran an indoor track schedule that consisted of four or more meets. 25% of our runners ran one or two indoor meets. The final 20% of our runners did not run indoor races. Meets ranged from indoor nationals to Monday evening fun meets at the local college. The only consistency with our runners and indoor track season is that there was no heavy interval workout period where they tapered and peaked for the indoor season. Training for the indoor meets consisted mostly of distance tempo runs peppered with small amounts of speed work.

Stretching
OK coaches hold on to your clipboards because stretching does not seem to make a significant difference in achieving our goal. 20% of our runners did no stretching, 25% of our runners did light stretching and a small majority of our runners did standard stretching before practice with two runners in that group also stretching after practice. The shakeout of whether faster runners stretched more compared to the others does not show a significant trend and, significantly, our state record holder fell into the light stretching category. I think we can attribute the non relevance of stretching to the fact that teenagers are just flexible by nature.

Diet
Other then filling up the tank with pasta on Friday night and having some food intake the morning of, there is no significant trend relating to eating habits.

Doubling Up at State
Much to my surprise, whether you doubled up at State does not make a difference. This statistic has a somewhat even split. 40% of our runners did not double and of the 60% that did double, half ran the 800 and the other half ran the 3200 m. We can find no consistent trend of

whether doubling up is good or bad for the 1600m. We even have some of our multiple year winners doubling up one year and running only one race the other year. There is no significant difference whether our runners doubled more often before 1980 when there was more time in between races. There may be some relevance that the 1600m is always the first distance race and doubling up may only become significant when determining the outcome of the second race. Another point that was not surveyed but may be relevant, is the fact that none of our runners mentioned they ran the four x 800 on Friday afternoon the day before the state mile.

Cross Training
Surprisingly, even in more recent years, we have no runners doing any cross training. Cross training was so absent from our survey, it might even be tempting to state that cross training could be detrimental to running. One thought here is that running is hard, exhausting work and there's not a lot of room for other time-consuming physical activities. Our final conclusion for cross training is similar to weight training; if it feels good do it, but we're not going to achieve any advantage.

What Age You Start Running
Good news for coaches and runners. You can jump into this game late and you do not need several years of running to make our goal. Our average runner started competing in seventh-grade. However, one of our runners did not start track until his junior year and several other runners did not run consistently throughout the previous seasons. What this category shows is that no matter when you start running it is not until your training follows the "what's important category" that you will be capable of running our 4:11. We'll discuss this more in our final conclusion.

Ohio High School State Mile Champions

What's Important

Here is the list of all the training factors our runners had in common. These are the training points and effort levels that, once our individual runners conformed to, they successfully performed at a level necessary to win the State 1600m title.

Again, this "what's important" list is based solely on the interviews with the runners and not on what anyone, including coaches and the author, may think is important to training for and winning the state 1600m.

Tapering

With the exception of our two winners in the 1960's, all of our runners tapered. Tapering for the most part consisted of reducing intervals and mileage for one or two weeks before the state meet. Typically, during the taper period, the speed of the intervals was increased. Tapering almost universally consisted of running short fast intervals and reducing mileage by 1/2 the volume.

Some of the classic questions with tapering are: when do we start tapering, how much do I cut back on volume of miles, and what type of speed work or sharpening intervals during the tapering period. Let us first look at what the majority of our runners did in response to these questions. In regards to when they started tapering, 50% of the our runners tapered for one week before the state meet, another 33% tapered two weeks before state and the last 15% tapered three weeks before state. Concerning volume of miles run during a week, 50% reduced their volume by one third, running approximately 35 miles a week during tapering. 25% reduced their volume by a half, another 25% reduced their volume by a quarter. As to interval or sharpening, the majority ran 200m to 400m intervals. Two runners ran no sharpening intervals, and one runner ran 800m repeats. Summarizing what we should do for tapering by based on what the majority of our runners did, we should taper only one week before state and run two sharpening workouts consisting of 200 to 400m repeats at a faster speed and run only a half-dozen of these. Our mileage would be reduced by a third, running approximately 30 to 35 miles for the tapering week.

But let's look at tapering from another angle. The purpose of tapering is to reduce effort levels of training and produce a faster race time. So let us try to draw a conclusion about tapering by reviewing just the runners that had their fastest time at the state meet. The runners that tapered and produced their fastest time at the state meet used the following tapering methods: they reduced volume of mileage by 50%,

78

tapered only one week before state and ran very few, if any, intervals. So we can conclude from the methods used by the runners who posted their fastest time at state that running a short one week taper with a more dramatic drop-off of volume and intervals produces a greater reduction in race time. This short taper matches the recent studies (Bannister 1999) that shows that an eight day taper with a 50% third day reduction and a 75% sixth day reduction produces the most dramatic improvement in performance.

Also of note is that some of our "one week before state taper" runners continued their taper into national meets soon after the state meet such as John Ziskha and Mason Ward, moving them into the two week taper group.

Another caveat concerning tapering. If we need to qualify for state with a good race at Regional then we need to factor in a two week taper that starts the week of Regional, reducing volume by 25%, and then reducing the taper to 50% the week of state. Below is the average 1st and 3rd place time over the last four years in the state Regional meets. We include the 3rd place time since in most Ohio regions third place advances. However, the number advancing changes every year and differs for each region. Check the OHSAA Web site to find the correct qualifying place.

Regional	1st	3rd
Area 1	4:20	4:22
Area 2	4:16	4:19
Area 3	4:19	4:23
Area 4	4:17	4:20

Regional winning and third place average 1600m times from 2004 - 2007.

Winter Running
Running in the winter months is an absolute must. Only one of our runners did not run during the winter, and this one runner was on the varsity basketball team during the winter. Mileage ranged from 25 miles a week to 75 miles a week with an average of 45 miles a week. Runners for the most part ran every day of the week after January 1. There seemed to be two different periods in the winter running season. Before January 1 where the runners did lower mileage and ran every other day and after January 1 where the mileage was increased and they ran every day. Time taken off after the cross country season, where no running was done, ranged from two days to two months, but

the average was roughly two weeks. What's critical here is that come January 1 we need to be in shape and ready to run 45 miles a week, putting in a good effort every day.

Cross Country
Running cross country is an absolute must. All but one of our runners ran cross country in the fall. The one exception did not run cross country because it was not available at his high school. He also ran the slowest winning State time of the group. Our runners' success in competing in cross country varies from state champions to also-rans. One of our runners even reports that cross country was somewhat of a club sport at his school where they only ran 25 miles a week. The requirement here is that you run cross country. Tthe good news is we don't have to be state champions at it to win the 1600m.

Sunday Running
Taking Sunday off to rest after the Saturday meet is not a trait that will win you any state titles. You need to get out and run at least 8 miles. The average for the group was 9.5. Only one runner did not run on Sunday and he ran the slowest winning state mile time. Our runners carried out these runs anywhere from slow scenery watching runs to fast tempo runs. Many runners treated Sunday as a moderately hard workout day that they incorporated into their weekly workout schedule. For example, running hard on Sunday doing 6:00 to 6:30 mile pace, then taking Monday practice easy and coming back for a hard Tuesday dual meet.

Race Day Warm Up
Universally the runners warmed up 120 to 90 minutes before their race. No one ran more then 2 miles during this warm up. Almost all the runners jogged approximately a mile and a half 90 minutes before they raced, rested 30 minutes before the race, put on their spikes and stretched, then did a half dozen strides.

400m Speed
We don't need an outrageous amount of foot speed to run a 4:11 1600m. Encouraging news for those who aren't blessed with a lot of speed, because if you don't have it naturally, it is very hard to come by. While a few of our runners ran below 50 seconds for 400m, the average was 53 seconds, which is doable for almost all moderately coordinated runners. We even have the three-time Olympian whose fastest quarter in high school was only a 58. For statistical reasons, let's throw out the slowest time and affirm that we need to at least run a 56 second quarter to be able to run our 4:11 mile.

Height and Weight

We can almost throw out a required height. This is more encouraging news because, like natural speed, if we are not blessed with height there's not a lot we can do about it. Our runners range in height from 5'6" to 6'2" and the average was 5' 10". There seems to be no correlation between height and how fast our runners ran the mile. What is relevant here is the ratio of weight to height. If we divide our runners weight by their height in inches we come out with a standard ratio of 2 lbs. per inch. This only fluctuated 20% higher or lower throughout the range of runners. So we can say that there is a maximum threshold of 2.2 lbs. per inch.

Workouts

Here is the what, when and how of the workouts that our winners followed. This next section will comprise the meat and potatoes of our proposed workout routine to follow.

Intervals

I think everyone knows that interval workouts are required when training for middle distance track events. What may not be so obvious are the details of interval workouts. Here is what we learned from our runners about intervals.

- **How many weeks of intervals**
  Almost universally, our runners started intervals in late March or early April and finished the last half of May before the regional meet. This is consistent with conventional wisdom that you need eight weeks of interval training. Start the last week of March and finish the third week of May. The only variation here may be a ninth week of intervals into the week of Regionals if we are looking to peak for national meets past the state championship week.

- **How many days per week of intervals**
  All but two of our runners ran interval workouts twice a week. The exceptions are, Tom Rapp who ran three interval workouts a week and Alan Scharsu, our pure Lydiard trainer who ran only one interval workout a week. A note, after high school both Tom and Alan went on to run extremely well at Penn State where they were part of a stellar 4 x mile relay team.

- **What distance of intervals**
  Once again our runners speak with almost a universal voice, longer repeats the first part of the season, followed by short, fast repeats the second half of the season. For the longer distances, 75% of our runners use three quarter mile to half-mile repeats. 1000m repeats were very popular with 50% of the total group running them. 25% of our runners ran one mile repeats in the first half of the interval season. In the second half of the interval season repeats were reduced almost universally down to 400m and 200m repeats.

- **Speed, Speed, Speed**
  Our runners turned out to be speed freaks. 200m and 300m all-out intervals, 400m and 200m racing, half miles under two minutes, these guys loved the speed. So we are going to require that our training includes as many opportunities as possible to race and run sub 60 second quarter miles. Get an attractive girl sprinter to show you how to use a set of blocks, learn to run a complete race in lanes, and remember that the start is three commands not two. The goal here is to know the Fast, and make a 63 second quarter seem slow.

Tempo Runs

Low six minute mile pace for seven miles or more at least once a week during the track season. Sub seven minute mile pace for nine miles or more several times a week during the winter. All of our runners talked about roadwork at a specific pace. They had courses that they knew the mileage and they timed themselves on these courses. Methods included starting out at seven minute mile pace and finishing at six minute mile pace, running the same course faster every time it was run, or running with older runners who could keep up the pace. Find someone who can run at this faster pace. Slowing down and waiting up for teammates is not an option. During the track season our runners did this hard tempo run on Sunday or Monday early in the week.

"God does not play dice with the universe."
Albert Einstein

The Proof

Why is it reasonable to think that we can measure, weigh and count out the exact requirements needed to win the State 1600m race? And even after we have determined the minimum requirements needed to complete this effort what gives us proof that anyone out of a crowd is capable of achieving the goal upon completing the requirements? Well if we believe in Albert Einstein that nothing is random, and there is a rhyme and reason for everything, then we can continue on. Beyond what Al says, our State 1600m champions show that there is evidence to support the concept that almost anyone can win the State 1600m title by doing the right things.

One of the interview questions for our runners was what were the fastest mile times for each grade in your high school running career. The chart in this chapter shows the results of the answers. The average decrease in times junior year to senior year is five seconds. However, there are two runners that are far outside this average, Mark Grogan and Jake Edwards. Mark Grogan dropped 25 seconds off his 1600m time and Jake Edward's dropped 15 seconds off his. Now if we look back at the interviews for these two runners we notice that during their senior year they followed the necessary training steps compiled from our "what's important" training categories, such as running on Sunday, putting in 50 miles a week over the winter, doing speed intervals etc. These two runners show a clear improvement in times and reached their goal of running a 4:11, compared to their slower times when they were not following the "what's necessary" elements.

Same people, same talent, same physical features but a faster time. The only thing that changed was the training. We can even throw Clark Haley into this proof of concept category. Clark did not run track until this junior year and did not race a 1600m until his senior year when, like our other winners, he fulfilled all the training requirements in the "what's important" list.

Ohio High School State Mile Champions

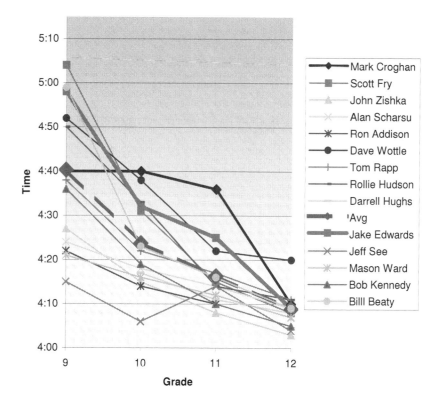

Chart showing fastest time per grade for State Champions

What is beautiful about having these three runners is that they validate our conclusion. They give us the faith and fortitude to put in the long miles during the winter, complete the hard intervals during the spring, the peace of mind to pull back during the tapering period, and the courage on the bell lap to empty the tank and win the race.

"Develop the base of several months of long aerobic runs, then begin interspersing several interval workouts per week while attempting to maintain the same mileage level. These interval workouts should be of varying distances from 220 through 880s, should start at gentle paces but cumulate too much sharper sessions as the runner approaches a targeted race. That's it. That's the only training you need to win a gold medal in the Olympics."
Marty Liquori

Training Schedule

Speed – lots of racing – hard tempo runs – running the same course over and over – watching the watch – hard short taper – mileage – visualizing the race – big base – mastering the breaking point. I had a lot of coaching and training concepts that got vaporized by this exercise. I also had a good number of beliefs that got verified.

So let us now put down on paper the training routine of the State 1600m champions. Remember, this is specific to running a 4:10 1600 meter on the first Saturday in June in Columbus, Ohio. Don't think less of this method because a world record holder or a NCAA champion did differently. Our goal is 4:10 not 3:50.

The Workout Schedule

We have shifted and sorted the details of our winners, and have determined the requirements needed for a six months and one week workout schedule. Here is where we lay out each month with daily practices.

There are four segments in the six-month routine that represent four different workout periods. First is the month of January, a light month of running slow distance with the goal of getting us ready to run the high mileage in the second segment. The second segment covers seven weeks starting February till the third week of March. This period of running is building the base of distance needed for sustaining us during the eight weeks of intervals, and this period contains the highest mileage of the season with mostly long runs and fast paced tempo runs. The third segment is eight weeks of interval workouts and regular season meets. The last period is the tapering in the two weeks leading up the state meet.

85

Ohio High School State Mile Champions

The following workout calendar shown is simplified into four weeks per month, not the actual four and a half weeks per month. To find the starting and ending point for the four different periods, we start with the first week in June and work backwards. Lay out your training segments by getting out a calendar of the current year, go to the first Saturday in June and mark off the two preceding weeks for the taper period. Next highlight the eight weeks before the two-week taper period for the interval workout segment. The first and second workout segments do not require an exact length of time like the third and fourth segments. The first segment will run the length of December. The second segment starts the first of January and lasts till the start of the third segment which was designated by working backwards ten weeks from the State meet in the first week of June.

Six months and a week. That's all we need to focus on. Here are the months laid out with the workouts. The value for each day is the running miles required. A blank day is a non running day.

December Workout

Week	Sunday	Monday	Tuesday	Wednesday	Thursday	Friday	Saturday	Week Miles	Effort Level
Dec 1		5	5	5		5	5	25	5
Dec 2	5	5	5		5	5		25	5
Dec 3	5	5		5	5		5	25	5
Dec 4	5		5	5	5		5	25	5

Easy running but the holidays and short daylight hours make this month of running more than an after thought. Keeping the mileage up to 25 per week and running at lease five days a week is the goal here. We need to be ready to run 50 miles a week come January. Don't worry about the pace, just get use to running in the cold.

Ohio High School State Mile Champions

January Workouts

Week	Sunday	Monday	Tuesday	Wednesday	Thursday	Friday	Saturday	Weekly Miles	Effort Level
Jan 1	5	5	5	5	5	5	5	35	6
Jan 2	9	6	7	7	7	7	7	50	7
Jan 3	10	6	7	6	7	7	7	50	7
Jan 4	11	6	6	7	7	7	6	50	7

The first month of hard running. A lot of miles, cold short days and the track season seems like a long way off. Mile pace should be 7:00 to 7:30 per mile. Do not let this month go without putting the miles in. We cannot do the hard fast intervals without building the base. These miles are like putting money in the bank that we can draw out during the April and May interval period. If the bank account is not full, the check is going to bounce come end of May.

Run with a GPS watch or smartphone running app for logging miles and keeping track of your pace.

February Workouts

Week	Sunday	Monday	Tuesday	Wednesday	Thursday	Friday	Saturday	Weekly Miles	Effort Level
Feb 1	12	5	7	7	7	7	5	50	7
Feb 2	10	6	7 Groghan's Hill Grunts	7	7	7	6	50	7
Feb 3	10	7	7 Groghan's Hill Grunts	8	8	5	Capital Univ High School Meet - 4	50	7
Feb 4	10	6	7	7 Kennedy's Pole Poppers	7	7	6	50	8

The second month of mileage base building. The only off days should be the heavy snow days when there is no room to run on the roads. Use a stationary bike, Nordic Track or elliptical machine for 60 minutes if the roads are unrunable. We have put the first of three indoor meets on the third weekend. The majority of our State champions ran indoor and averaged three indoor meets. Mile pace should be 6:00 to 6:30 per mile by the end of the month. Watch the watch and try to get faster as the weeks go by. We have one day a week hill workouts for a little speed and a little change of pace. The last week we start some fartleks, getting ready for the end of season indoor State meet.

How important is pushing faster paces on these runs? Michelle Thomas from Glen Este High School in Cincinnati, Ohio read this book and followed the process. She had always run distance workouts not aware of her mile pace. She then started logging mile splits and attributes "watching the watch" a major factor in winning two State titles her senior year in 2010 and 2011.

Ohio High School State Mile Champions

March Workouts

Week	Monday	Tuesday	Wednesday	Thursday	Friday	Saturday	Week Miles	Effort Level
March 1	6	8 Kennedy's Pole Poppers	8	8	6	Buckeye High School Qualifier - 4	50	7
March 2	6	8 Kennedy's Pole Poppers	8	8	4	OATCCC Indoor State Meet - 4	49	8
March 3	6	7 Groghan's Hill Grunts	8	8 Kennedy's Pole Poppers	6	5	49	7
March 4	6	Dual Meet – 5 1600m & 3200m 4:30 & 9:50	7	Interval – 8 Fry's One Mile Flyers	4	1st Outdoor Meet – 5 4:25 to 4:35 1600m	45	9

March, the first part is more base mileage building with the State indoor meet in the first and second weeks. Do not take these meets too seriously. Few of our runners trained during the winter with the goal of peaking and winning the big indoor meets. If you do well at the indoor meets, great. If we finish middle of the pack even better. Our goal is to win the State 1600m the first Saturday in June and the less other runners know where we are the better.

The third week we do two fast pace workouts getting ready for the first week of being on the track. The last week we have our first dual meet. Let's run the 1600m and 3200m in this dual, keep the mileage up and not blow any hamstrings in the cold weather. 1600m race times should be 4:35 to 4:25.

April Workouts

Week	Monday	Tuesday	Wednesday	Thursday	Friday	Saturday	Week Miles	Effort Level
April 1	10	6	Interval – 6 1000x4 @ 2:55 3 min rest	7	Interval – 8 Beaty's Two Man Basher	4	2nd Outdoor Meet – 5 4:30 1600m	45	10
April 2	10	6	Dual Meet – 5 4:25 1600m	6	Interval – 7 800m – 600m 800x3 @ 2:10 3 min rest	6	3rd Outdoor Meet - 5	45	9
April 3	10 See's Sunday Smoker	6	Interval – 6 600x6 @ 1:36 3 min rest	7	Interval – 8 600m – 400m 8x400@ 64 2 min rest	4	4th Outdoor Meet – 5 low 4:20s 1600m	45	10
April 4	10	6	Dual Meet – 5 Olympic Dual Meet Masochist	6	Interval – 7 Poole's Cinder Pounders	6	5th Outdoor Meet - 5	45	9

April might be the hardest month of the six. Hard intervals, dual meets, Saturday invitationals and keeping the miles up. Early in the month intervals are longer – 600s, 800s and up. The second half of the season intervals come down to 200s and 400s. Keep the mileage tempo runs around 6:00 mile pace. Do not get discouraged if our 1600m times are not in the teens or even in the twenties. You cannot race and train at the same time. 1600m race times should be 4:30 to 4:20.

If you do not have a Tuesday dual meet, run a workout for that day similar to the Thursday of that week.

Ohio High School State Mile Champions

May Workouts

Week	Monday	Tuesday	Wednesday	Thursday	Friday		Saturday	Week Miles	Effort Level
May 1	10	6	Interval – 6 600x6 @ 1:36 3 min rest	7	Interval – 8 400m 8x400@61 2 min rest	4 Ward's Friday Wakeup	6th Outdoor Meet - 5	45	10
May 2	10	6	Interval - 7 Husdon's Half Dozen	6	Interval – 7 300m – 400m 8x400@61 2 min rest	4	League Meet - 5	45	9
May 3	10 See's Sunday Smoker	6	Interval – 6 300m – 400m 9x300@45 2min rest	5	Interval – 6 200m – 300m 10x200@28 1.5 min rest	4	District Meet – 4 4:19	42	7
May 4	6	5	6	5	5 Zishka's 300m Zapers	4	Regional Meet – 4 4:16	35	5
June 1	6	4 Zishka's 300m Zapers	3	3	3	3	State Meet – 3 4:11	25	3

May and it's time to see the plan coming to completion. See's Sunday Smoker is the long last hard tempo run of the season. The mileage runs on the last week of May are 6:30 per mile pace. State week is our hard drop taper. Go slow and easy and trust the past winners. 1600m race times should be low 4:20s. Tapering should reduce that race time by 3% or 8 seconds giving us a 4:11 for State meet.

The Lord will afflict your knees and legs with pain that cannot be cured, spreading from the soles of your feet to the top of your head.
Deuteronomy 28:35

Workouts of the Champions
Here are the workouts seeded throughout the training calendar shown in the previous section. These workouts come straight from the champions. They will put hair on your chest and make a man out of you. If you can do these workouts you will fear no one on the track. Don't worry if the first time you run them you can't complete them. Run them a second or third time until you get through them.

Getting to the next level of effort and speed is what these workouts are all about. This is truly where the winning is done. Remember the pain is passing and the workouts only last 60 minutes. Also remember that the third part of any workout or race is the hard part mentally. This is the period when you have to forget the last lap, close your eyes, take a deep breath and mash on the gas pedal. Don't worry about the last quarter, it will take care of itself.

Stated effort level is 1 to 10, with ten being a near death experience and a heart rate up above 160.

Poole's Cinder Pounders
Mid Season Workout – Effort 9
Old school on the cinders. Eight 440yd repeats at 62 seconds with 3 minutes break. With no bounce, a lot of foot slip on your push off and 4 yards longer than the 400m these 62s are more like 59s. Cinder tracks make you push constantly to keep your speed up, no coasting here. If it's a windy day and you lose form at the end, the track will grow hands that grab your ankles. You'll struggle to do 65s. But the plus side is when you get back on the rubber you will feel like superman.

Note, when looking for an old cinder track, make sure you have a 440yd track not a 400yd track. A tip off is that on a 400yd track the football field end zones run onto the curves. 400yd tracks are ok to use just add 40yds to the end of one complete lap. Use the football field yard marking to measure off the additional 40 yds. Also, no cheating by wearing spikes.

93

Ohio High School State Mile Champions

Beaty's Two Man Basher
Early to Mid Season Workout – Effort 10
Two guys and 40 quarters, a hell of a way to spend an afternoon. It's a two man 10 mile relay. Each man runs 20 quarters at 70 seconds each. Rest periods are the 70 seconds when the other guy is running. If you don't like your relay partner, try running a faster quarter and shortening his rest time.

300m Zishka Zapers
Taper Week – Effort 4
John is the fastest miler in the history of Ohio high school track and here is one of his tapering workouts. Run five 300m as fast as you can with a 5 to 6 minute rest in between them, almost a complete recovery. Be careful this is taper week. Do not shorten the rest time, extend it if you are not rested before the next repeat. We want the speed not the effort.

Husdon's Half Dozen
MidSeason – Effort 9
Speed. Speed. Speed. 6 to 8 x 400m repeats at 55 seconds with a one minute rest. This is how Rollie made the 62-64 seconds 400m laps needed to win State not seem so fast. Do less if needed to keep the speed up. This is a high effort workout and you should be tightening up and rigging on the last 2 to 3. Concentrate on good form, posture and speed.

Groghan's Hill Grunts
PreSeason or Early Season – Effort 7
Find a hill on the grass that is 100 meters or more long. It must also be steep enough to sled down. After warming up a couple of miles run a dozen fast strides up this hill. There is no walking during this workout and the recovery period between repeats should be just the jog down the hill. If possible, find a longer route down the hill so as to avoid running down too steep of a slope.

Ward's Friday Wakeup
Early to MidSeason – Effort 5
While standard practice is to rest on the Fridays before Saturday meets, Mason would run a moderate road workout on Fridays. Run six miles on a flat road course. Run 6:00 to 6:30 per mile and make sure you run during the day. Running this workout late Friday evening will not allow you to recover for Saturday afternoon racing.

See's Sunday Smoker
Any Time Except Taper Weeks – Effort 8
10 miles on the road on Sunday. Start these 10 miles runs around 7 or 7:15 minute miles pace and by the end of the run work down to 6:30-6:15 minute mile pace. Try the same course each Sunday and lower your times each week.

Kennedy's Pole Poppers
PreSeason – Effort 7
A great way to break up all the mileage runs in the winter. During road runs of six miles or more start running pickups from telephone pole to telephone pole. Pole to pole pickups should be longer than one minute in length and no logger than two minutes. Also a great way to get some speed in for those indoor meets. Important note, do not let the pickups and the recovery jogs to turn into the same speed. Keep the speed up on the pickup and slow down on the recovery jog.

Fry's One Mile Flyers
Early Season – Effort 9
Just four, one mile repeats. Warm up a couple of miles and then head to the track. These mile cutdown workouts consist of four 1 mile repeats starting at 4:50 pace and ending up at 4:30 or better. Take a five minute rest in between. The last two are where the damage is done and the 3rd one is mentally the toughest to keep the speed up. Work hard on the third one and forget about the last one until you run it.

Olympic Dual Meet Masochist
Early and Midseason – Effort 9
Popular with the Olympic runners in our group, these are a great way to do a speed workout and gain race experience. In a midweek dual meet run the 1600m, 400m, 800m and 200m, then end with the 4x400m. Do not anchor the last leg of the 4x400m, your tank should be empty at this point and it will not be a pretty race. Your teammates will not be happy if they put you in the lead only to see you stampeded under foot in the last 100 meters.

Racing Strategy

She blinded me with science
As sweet as any harmony
She blinded me with science
And failed me in geometry
She Blinded Me with Science - Thomas Dolby

Proposed Mile Race Strategy for Best Performance
Mile and 1600m races up to the 4:30 performance level.

- Is there an optimal method and strategy for racing the high school mile?

- Why have there been so many sub 4:05 high school milers and only a handful of sub 4:00 high school milers?

- What can we learn from looking at the sub 4:00 high school performances?

Now that we have analyzed and created our conditioning and training for an optimum mile performance let's look at the best method for actually performing this task. Let's determine the best method for running a mile in the shortest amount of time. To do this we will follow our method of examining previous successful endeavors and extracting from them key elements, but we will also review another inescapable truth of how the human body performs during a mile race and what are the conditions and limits on this performance. For this second analytical review we will take from the standard knowledge base of athletic physiology. We will follow are tried-and-true mode of taking existing facts and weeding out opinions. Our assumptions on the energy creation during the activity of running are all well accepted standards that were proven out through clinical studies in the 1960s and 70s.

96

Three Stages of Energy Production While Running

The first few seconds of any strenuous activity energy is created from anaerobic breakdown of muscle glycogen and blood glucose. This is a oxygenless system that operates until the aerobic system starts producing energy. This anaerobic energy creation produces lactic acid. A runner can operate approximately 2 minutes on this anaerobic energy source

The second source of energy is from an aerobic energy creation this is converting muscle and liver glycogen by the use of oxygen. This is a highly efficient energy creation method that does not create lactic acid. By product of this phase 2 aerobic energy creation is water and carbon dioxide.

The anaerobic and aerobic energy source creation can operate simultaneously. The anaerobic energy creation will take over when the aerobic energy creation cannot keep pace with the requirements.

Lactic acid buildup requires several minutes and liters of oxygen to remove from the blood system. Buildup of lactic acid and heavy energy creation from anaerobic source is called going into oxygen debt.

Third energy source is an aerobic system that utilizes body fat to create energy. This energy creation requires more oxygen and is less efficient. This third energy source of burning body fat for energy creation is utilized in marathon and other long-distance races. This aerobic energy creation from fat can be a partial replacement for carbohydrate anaerobic energy creation. The fat burning aerobic phase is the reason so many middle-distance runners engage in marathon type training during at least part of the season. The more the body can be trained to burn fat the longer can forestall the completion of its glycogen.

The Gears Used in the Mile

Marty Liquori considers these phases of energy creation and how the body uses them during a race in similar terms of a car with gears. With one of these stages of energy being the primary gear that the runner utilizes at one given time. So if we think about a race and using our body to create energy similar to a car with three gears and each gear has a separate gas tank. Our fastest gear is our anaerobic gear that utilizes blood glycogen. It creates extremely high level of energy needed for sprinting however it creates lactic acid which slows the system down and it's gas tank is only good for 60-90 seconds of use. The near gear can be considered our primary gear. This is the aerobic burning of glucose in the blood system. This gear is our main gear and has enough in the gas tank to last 90 minute or more and creates no lactic acid which can slow our system down. The third gear creates energy off our stored fat cells and can be thought of as a failover system. Our bodily creates energy with this gear when our second gear, aerobic energy gear hits it's limit due to the amount of oxygen it can burn. Running hard enough aerobically, that we overextend beyond our second gear the body starts to burn fat to supplement this loss of energy. Burning fat in gear three has a gas tank that is as big is the amount of fat were storing, it does not create lactic acid buildup and is the least efficient at creating energy.

Now that we know we have three gears to use a race and we know how fast each one of these gears can drive our body and we know how big the gas tank is attached to each gear we can start to plan our energy consumption race plan. This plan will look to maximize each gear making sure that we finished the race with the first two gas tanks on empty and using that gas in the most efficient way to create the fastest race.

Mile Race Strategy

Let's go through a proposed race with this new strategy. The gun goes off and we have a short sprint to find our position. Key to this phase of the race is to utilize as little anaerobic energy production is possible. We do not want to create lactic acid in the first 200m of the race that will cause us to underperform because the oxygen can't flow in highly acidic blood. Using this anaerobic gear any time during the first ¾ of the race needs to be eliminated or best minimize to seconds. After the first hundred or 200 yards we settle into a second gear - aerobic energy creation. Our maximum speed in this gear is dependent on our VO2max level. We will plan on running the next 800 to 1000 meters using this second gear. Reaching a third stage of our race somewhere between 900 m and 1300m will start to overtax our aerobic second-gear. This is the third lap and is the classic hardest and slowest lap. We now have anywhere from 400m to 200m to go and we switch over to our first gear of anaerobic energy. This is where we exert maximum effort over the last approximately 300m creating high amounts of energy and building up lactic acid quickly. We must time this last gear change so that our lactic acid buildup is not so great in the last hundred meters that the bear hops on our back. If all goes according to plan we've run our fastest possible mile, we used all three of our gears,

Our gas tanks are empty and our body is completely saturated with lactic acid.

Proof

Now let's look at this proposed theory and see if we can get any proof by looking at our sub four-minute milers. We'll take all of our high school sub four-minute mile performances and chart each lap split by each runner. The chart produced shows that all our runners are very consistent in their lap speeds using these gears. We start out with a quick sprint using the anaerobic gear, we quickly settle into our aerobic pace, third lap slows a little when we start to bump up against our VO2max level, and back to the first gear in our fourth lap which utilizes our fastest speed where we have our quickest lap on our way to a sub 4 minute mile.

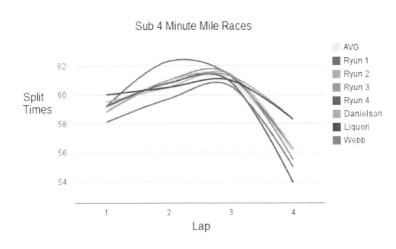

Sub 4 Minute Mile Races

Lap	Ryun 1	Ryun 2	Ryun 3	Ryun 4	Danielson	Liquori	Webb	AVG	avg w/o fastest 2
1	59.2	59.5	58.8	59.2	58.8	60.0	58.1	59.09	59.26
2	62.3	60.5	61.0	60.8	61.0	60.5	59.7	60.83	61.00
3	61.3	61.4	61.4	60.9	61.3	61.0	60.6	61.13	61.28
4	56.2	56.2	55.5	53.9	58.3	58.3	55.0	56.20	56.90
finish		3:58.1	3:56.8	3:55.3	3:59.4	3:59.8	3:53.43	3:57.24	3:58.5

Ohio High School State Mile Champions

Proposed Mile Race for Lowest Effort and Best Performance

Combining the two sources of data, what science tells us about energy creation at the mitochondria level and what our sub four-minute high school milers have accomplished, let's create the optimum race strategy for running a sub four-minute mile.

Looking at quarter mile splits for our previous performances let's calculate the average for each quarter-mile. But before we do that let's look at removing the two fastest times. Jim Ryun's 3:55 and Alan Webb's 3:53 miles are so far beyond our goal of 3:59 that were going to remove them. This takes us to the last column on the table above where we average the quarter miles without these two fastest times. We start out with a 59 second quarter, followed by a 61 second quarter, Followed by another slower 61 second quarter, and then finishing off with a 57 second quarter. This strategy follows very nicely our physiological process of energy creation. An initial use of muscle glycogen into an aerobic state for a quick first quarter-mile followed by a slight slowing down over the next two laps when we go into our aerobic blood glycogen use, followed by our fastest quarter-mile effort using all our anaerobic energy during the last 200 to 300 yards kick.

The only slight variable on this race strategy is when do we begin our final kick, timing it correctly so that we consume all our blood glycogen but not over extend the effort and empty this gas tank before the finish line. If we again refer to our previous successful attempts and historically look back on these races we find that the majority of the runners started to pick up the pace with approximately 300 meters to go and then began an all-out sprint with approximately 100 yards to go. Jim Ryun's multiple successful high school sub four-minute miles show this in the extremely well-documented book "The Jim Ryun Story" by Nelson. Ryun's high school coaches were fanatical about recording every hundred meter split during Jim's mile races.

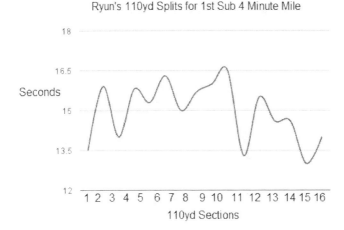

Ryun's 110yd Splits for 1st Sub 4 Minute Mile

110yd Sections

The table above shows Jim Ryun's first sub four-minute mile at the Compton Relays. Ryan spreads out his final kick over the last quarter-mile and his fastest hundred yards over the last lap happens with 200 yards to go not over the last hundred yards.

Optimum Splits for Mile Performances above 4 Minutes

Now let's extend this race strategy to fit a broader group of high school runners, those looking to run a 4:10, a 4:20 and a 4:30 minute mile. The table below shows the 440yd splits for each one of these goals. To find these splits we extended each quarter by the straight percentage of the final time against the original 3:58.5 splits in the previous table. The table below shows these calculated 440yd splits for each one of the selected races.

4:10.0	4:20.0	4:30.0
62.12	64.60	67.09
64.00	66.56	69.12
64.23	66.80	69.37
59.64	62.03	64.42

101

Ohio High School State Mile Champions

What Next?

Two questions that may arise out of this proposed racing strategy are the following; Can this mile race strategy be applied to other similar races such as the half-mile with the two-mile? And what do we do about other competitors and their presence and actions during a race that may interfere with our perfect race strategy? The answer to the first question is no, the mile is specific in the time it takes to run - 4 minutes. This is very different than a half mile which takes 2 minute to run and does not rely as much upon our aerobic ability. As for the two-mile, specific to high school speeds, it is not as fast as the mile and does not require the close monitoring of an aerobic energy production as the mile does. The mile is very specific because of the speed at which it is run and the time it takes to cover that distance. The answer to our second question about competing against other runners during will be answered in a following chapter as we lay out the three laws of racing the mile.

Three Laws of Racing the Mile

Rule 1 - Use the gears, it's not an automatic

We have already detailed this strategy in the previous chapter (How to race the mile), and it is our first rule of racing the mile. We'll name this the Marty Liquori law after he used the term in his 1980 book. The rule is; the first and the last lap are faster than the middle two, and the last lap is faster than the first lap. I received a confirmation on this rule soon after I showed it to Tom Rapp, coach of Mason High School, Ohio. Not only does Tom have one of the fastest mile performances for high schoolers, he also coaches some of the fastest high school milers in the nation.

"This generally bears out my rule of thumb which has been:
Laps 1 and 4 - 2 seconds faster than pace.
Laps 2 and 3 - 2 seconds slower than pace"

We have analyzed the optimum pace and lap splits for running the mile, but how is that affected by other runners on the track during our race? How do we deal with other runners while trying to perform our ultimate race? We have all heard the many different race strategies; stay behind the leaders then kick, stay out of traffic in the back, surge at different points, take the lead on a specific lap. Every coach has his favorite and every runner has his own. But are there any rules that we can use as guidelines that can assure us the best possible results? We know of no documented rules for racing the mile, so let's try and uncover some.

Rule 2 - Don't jockey unless you are riding a horse

After watching dozens of old mile racing videos on YouTube I started to notice a trend of runners that jockeyed back and forth through the field never won or even made it to the podium. To test this observation up I took the last five Olympic 1500m men's finals and tracked the top seven finishers for each race. I counted how many times each runner passed another runner. The Olympic races were chosen with the thinking that these world class runners would use the best possible racing strategy. The results are quite revealing.

Ohio High School State Mile Champions

Passing vs Placing

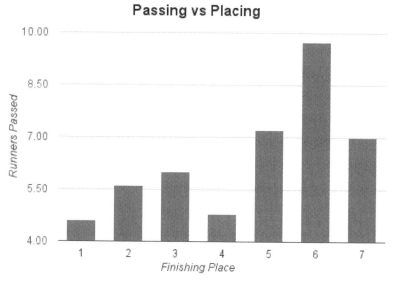

On average the runners that finished in 5th, 6th and 7th places passed twice as many runners that finished in the top three places. The winners passed on average only 4.6 runners during the race. The 6th place runners passed average of 9.5 runners. Watching and logging the passing metrics on these races you start to notice very quickly that the winners would quickly settle into mid pack by the first 200m and then just sit there till their final kick. Runners that would start up front then slide back and then surge back to the front were always doomed. Runners that started in the back then mid race sprinted to the front finished with the same poor results. The top three finishers were steady mid pack runners that sat on the inside lane and made only one move to the front.

If we take our two fastest high school mile performances, Ryun's 3:55 and Webb's 3:53, they serve as perfect examples of our second rule. Both high school runners, competing in world-class events with the top milers of the day started the race in the back, completing the first two laps in close to last place, never exerting themselves or passing other runners. The third lap they slowly and methodically work their way up to the front third of the competitors, never passing the same runner twice. The last lap was their fastest trip around the track, passing runners while never being passed themselves.

Webb's Record run: www.youtube.com/watch?v=niCWRb29y-E

A corollary of our second law could be stated as "do not pass the same runner twice." The second law itself could be thought of as a sub of our first law, using our gears wisely and conserving energy.

Rule 3 - Don't play the lotto unless you hold the winning ticket

Ok, we have our pace and lap splits, we have a plan for managing the other runners. Now only one big question left - what about the kick? When do we kick, how fast, do we play it by ear or plan a specific point to start kicking. Once again, let's follow the success of others.

If we look at our sub4 high schoolers and add in Olympic 1500m winners we can see a clear trend. Winners started picking up the pace with 300m to go, moving from mid pack to the front or close to it. Then, anywhere from 200 to 150 meters to go let go with their all out sprint to the finish. And this sprint was not a fast stride or a 80% top speed, this was an all out top speed effort.

There are some great examples of this two stage kick. One of the most dramatic examples of this strategy was Peter Snell's 1964 Tokyo win. Snell was determined to pick up the pace with 300m to go, but was severely boxed in, up against the curb with runners in front beside and behind him. At this moment he throws his right arm out, moving the other runners out of the way as he unboxes himself and moves to the front. With 200m to go he breaks into a full sprint and wins by one of the biggest margins in the history of the 1500m.

Snell's 1500m Kick: www.youtube.com/watch?v=kVJQoo70Lic

Key to this successful strategy over the last lap is picking up the pace 50 to 100 yards into the last lap. Jim Ryun describes this increase in speed the following way describing his last lap performance of his record-setting 3:55 mile. "At the 330 I caught up with Odlozil and went by him as hard as I could, not quite going all out, knowing I had enough left for a good finish." Runners following Ryun were Peter Snell, the other was American mile record holder Jim Grelle. Snell and Grelle mimicked Ryun's two-stage kick but could not pass him in the last 300 yards. Jim began his final all-out kick after gaining the lead on the backstretch, with 200 yards to go. Holding off both Snell and Grelle by a 10th and 2 tenths at the tape. Ryun's last lap heroics were not spur the moment strategies.

Ohio High School State Mile Champions

Ryun and his high school coaches were meticulous about planning races. Here is a recount from Nelson's 1968 biography of how Ryun and his high school coach Jim Edmiston planned for the historic rematch race against Peter Snell.

On Sunday afternoon, Jim and Coach Edmiston lay on their beds in their motel room and planned the race.

Jim was well aware of his mistakes in the past. His two major errors were running wide and letting others get the jump on him on the last backstretch.

Running wide forced him to run further, for each foot out from the curb added an extra 3 ft. around one turn. He would correct this error by staying back, on the pole, during early going where his main purpose was to conserve energy. When it came time to pass a runner, he would do it decisively instead of running alongside.

The second mistake was more difficult to correct. It would be easy enough for him to get the jump on others. All he had to do is start sooner. But if he started to soon he would not be able to his kick all the way to the finish. Therefore, they planned it so that Jim would move up into position with a lap and a half to go. Then, just before the last backstretch, he would quickly move into the lead. They felt 300 yd. was too long for him to sprint, so soon after he took the lead he was to wait until Snell tried to pass him then he would sprint.

The accuracy and exactly correct speculation of how the race would unfold and how Ryun would perform on the last lap is amazing. It shows us that having a plan and following the plan can succeed. The rule of thumb here is not to be emotional and try to wing it - playing the Lotto is for suckers, planning around real world conditions and known variables is the smart bet.

Ryun outkicking Snell: www.youtube.com/watch?v=_E-R97LShwA

Marty Liquori the High School Years
Training and Racing June 1967

June 1967 Marty Liquori was a high school senior 2800 miles from his New Jersey home running the big California track meets. Looking to become the third American high schooler to break the 4 minute mile, Marty would make his goal on June 23rd running in what most believe was the greatest mile ever run on a US track - the 1967 AAU Nationals in Bakersfield. Seven runners in that race would break the four minute barrier and the winner, Jim Ryun, would lower his own world record to 3:51.1.

Liquori's sub 4 mile: www.youtube.com/watch?v=xlwS0Fyq8vk

The following is a brief interview with Marty about his high school training and his running log book transcribed form that May and June of 1967.

Marty Liquori - Essex Catholic High School - Newark, NJ
Interviewed Dec 2012

Marty's high school track coach was the accomplished runner Fred Dryer who attended Villanova University and held numerous national running titles. Fred's college coach at Villanova was Jim "Jumbo" Elliott who would also be Marty's future college coach at Villanova.

Marty had a lot of physical activity when he was a kid. He played baseball and basketball in grade school and rode his bike to basketball practice and most other places. In his words there was no free rides, no carpools and his dad would've laughed at him had he asked for a transportation to a sports practice event.

Marty did not run the mile his freshman year. This is because freshman were not allowed to run that distance. Marty first ran the mile his sophomore year and his best time was 4:17.1. He was injured his junior year but still managed to run a 4:13. His senior year best mile was his 3:59.8 performance.

Cross Country

Marty came in 2nd at the prestigious Eastern State's race in Van Cortland Park his junior year. The next year he won that same race, and set a course and meet record of 12:23.2 on the 2 ½ mile course. Fred Dwyer was also Marty's cross country coach in high school.

Ohio High School State Mile Champions

Training

Marty ran on Sunday's 12 to 15 miles. He would run for an hour and 45 min. He did not pay attention to the mileage just the time. Marty ran with a watch, not to pace his miles, but to run for a total set length of time. In his words they were performed at a fairly easy pace. Marty recalls 7 min. mile pace for these runs. Marty also ran with a transistor radio while he did his long runs. He did not run the same course every Sunday. His mileage was 70 miles per week year-round.

Interval workouts

Marty did interval workouts three days a week. Monday the intervals were longer 8x800, Marty comments that the intervals he did were pretty basic stuff such as 15x440, also 220s. Interval days were Monday, Tuesday and Thursday. Fridays before meets were easy distance runs. Marty keep a log of all his high school workouts and continued to keep diaries for every year he ran.

Marty comments that he did not have a lot of leg speed when compared to Jim Ryun. He does not have a exact time for a competitive performance quarter-mile but he does estimate that he would probably be able to run a 52nd quarter-mile in high school going off his ability that to run a 48 second quarter-mile in college. His fastest half-mile in high school was a 1:51 that he ran during the leg of a relay. In bigger meets Marty rarely doubled up.

Marty started running twice a day more consistently when he was a senior in high school, this was facilitated by his new driver's license and ability to have time to run in the morning, instead of riding the public bus for an hour to get to school. He typically did 3 to 5 miles on these morning runs. This pushed him up over 12 miles a day.

His high school workouts were built along the KISS model "Keep It Simple Stupid." Fred Dywer would design workouts like 5x880 or 12x440 with the same amount of distance jog recovery. This differed from when Marty was out of college and he followed a more advanced style training where intervals during one workout were mixed, running 200's, 400's and 800's during one practice session.

Marty's high school did not have a track and their interval workouts were done at a nearby park where a white line drawn around trees to designated an approximate quarter-mile. The course included exposed

108

tree roots and a backstretch that had an inclined matched by a front stretch that had a decline. Their high school did have an indoor wooden track that was typical of East Coast parochial schools.

Tapering

Fred Dywer had Marty tapering the last four weeks of the season before big events. Marty firmly believes that current runners do not taper for a long enough period of time. He believes that two weeks is the minimum and four weeks is optimal for the body to react properly to the conditioning and tapering process. Marty averaged 50 miles a week for the last two months of the track season.

In the 70s The President's Council On Physical Fitness printed a pamphlet that contained both Marty and Jim Ryun's workouts. There is a typo in this book that states Marty's Monday workouts were 16x800, this is incorrect it should be 8x800. Marty recounts a story of a young runner approaching him to autograph his pamphlet and the young runner mentions to Marty that his Monday workouts were really impressive and that no one on his team could do a similar work out. Marty then mentions that yes, 8x800 repeats was a hard workout, and the boy replies no it's 16x880, and Marty says no the workout was 8 x 880s and the young man replies no look here in the book. Marty looks in the book and sees the type that states 16x880s on Monday and 16x440s on Tuesday. "So all these high school kids and coaches that I imagine did know a thing about training were trying to do work out that no one could possibly do in high school."

How To Train For The Mile

by Marty Liquori
(current AAU and NCAA Mile champion)

If you were born with a big heart and superior cardiovascular system, you've got half the battle licked in trying to become a four minute miler. Because milers spend two-thirds of their training time trying to increase the efficiency of their cardiovascular system. A miler should run anywhere from 80 to 120 miles per week in the early months of yearly training cycle. This long distance running begins in July and runs through September when the cross country season begins.

Don't skip the cross country season. It's important for a miler to compete during September, October, and November in these 2½ to 5 mile meets. Work hard right up to the big races and then rest the week prior so you can be strong for the actual race. Many runners make the mistake of running too hard too close to the actual race. *Don't be running when you should be resting.*

Vary your distance running in the fall with interval training on the track. Try this workout.

Distance	Target Time	Number of Repetitions	Total Mileage
½ mi.	2:15	16-20	8-10
¼ mi	:65	20	5

A daily workout routine in the fall should break down like this.

Morning	Afternoon	Evening
5 mile run	10-12 miles	Weight Training
	(Vary routine,	(1) Bench Presses, 155
	run intervals on	lbs., 4 reps, 6 sets
	track two days a	(2) Arm Curls, 90 lbs.,
	week and continuous	4 reps, 6 sets
	running on other days.)	2 MINUTE REST PERIOD
		BETWEEN SETS

A general rule to follow in training for the mile is to increase your speed workouts as you approach the outdoor track season. For instance, as I move closer to the spring months, I run my interval routines at better than race tempo. For example, I aim for 57 seconds or less in running my ¼ mile repeats.

Cardiovascular Fitness

As I said in my introduction, milers spend most of their time developing the cardiovascular system. The relationship is simple: the more miles you run, the more efficient your circulatory and respiratory

Marty's running log book transcribed from May and June of 1967.
Marty Liquori - Essex Catholic High School - Newark, NJ

Day	Date	Workout/race
Friday	April 28	30x220
Saturday	April 29	15 miles 2pm
Sunday	April 30	15 miles
Monday	May 1	10 miles
Tuesday	May 2	7 miles
Weds	May 3	14 - weights - swim
Thurs	May 4	15x300 - 8 miles
Friday	May 5	20x300 - 5 miles
Saturday	May 6	20x300 - 8 miles
Sunday	May 7	8 miles
Monday	May 8	20x300 - 5 miles
Tuesday	May 9	25x350 - 5 miles
Weds	May 10	15x220 yds
Thurs	May 11	11 miles - weights
Friday	May 12	12 miles
Saturday	May 13	4:32 mile
Sunday	May 14	16 miles
Monday	May 15	5x880 @ 2:15 - 5x220 - 5x1 block
Tuesday	May 16	12x440@63
Weds	May 17	5x880@2:08
Thurs	May 18	12x440
Friday	May 19	10 miles
Saturday	May 20	5x880 2:06
Sunday	May 21	8 miles
Monday	May 22	12x440@63 last one 56
Tuesday	May 23	25x330@56
Weds	May 24	10 miles 5:30 per mile - 2 miles jog
Thurs	May 25	330's
Weds	May 26	10 x 440 @ 59
Friday	May 26	8 miles
Sat	May 27	2 mile race @ 9:04.7. at St Joesph Montvale NJ - Hot no spikes - 64 - 2:24 - 4:32 -70 - 70 9:04, 62 last 1/4, 29 last 220 10 x 220 5 mile jog
Sun	May 28	10 x 440 58, 59, 59, 60, 61, 62, 62 62, 61, 67 10 x 220
Monday	May 29	off
Tues	May 30	4 miles
Weds	May 31	4 miles

Ohio High School State Mile Champions

Thurs	June 1	4 miles
Friday	June 2 - 8:30 Colisium	4:01.1mile 58 -2:02.5 - 3:03 - 58. Jim Ryun won 3:53 2nd fast of all time. got nipped at the tape by John Lawson we both had the same time - 4:1.1. Good last 220 beat Rick Romero, Tim Danielson
Saturday	June 3	7 miles
Sunday	June 4	12 x 440 @65
Monday	June 5	8 x 220 - 8 x 440. Alternating 64 sec 440 with a 30 sec 220
Tues	June 6	5 x 880 2:04 - 2:03 - 2:04
Weds	June 7	10 strides on grass - 5 miles
Thurs	June 8	off
Friday	June 9	off
Saturday	June 10	4:00.1 mile. 10pm I led the first 440 in 62, Danielson took it thru a 2:02 880. I out kicked both Dave and Tim and won in 4:00.1
Sunday	June 11	1 hour
Monday	June 12	1 hour + 1/2
Tues	June 13	3 x - 3x 880 2:03.9 - 2:04 - 2:06 1 x 440 3 x 220 Felt bad
Weds	June 14	10x440 under 64 striding and jogging
Thurs	June 15	50 minute run
Friday	June 16	Rest
Sat	June 17	Night Golden West 62 - 2:06 - 3:08 - 4:08 1st place - 4 miles
Sun	June 18	5 miles 10x220 4 miles
Monday	June 19	6x440
Tues		NA
Weds	June 21	jog whirlpool
Thurs	June 22	qualilying 64 - 2:09 - 3:09 - 4:08.7
Friday	*June 23*	*8:45pm 59.8 - 2:00 - 3:01.8 - 3:59.8. A Sub 4:00 Miler - Jim Ryun Worlds Record 3:51.1 3 guys went 3:56 I was 7th*
Saturday	June 24	No Sleep No Run
Sunday	June 25	Surprise party 5 miles
Monday	June 26	7 miles
Tuesday	June 27	off
Weds	June 28	7 miles on beach
Thurs	June 29	5 miles on beach
Friday	June 30	8x440 - 4x100yds

This scanned image from Marty's log of the Bakersfield meet at the bottom of this page. Marty's statement of " A Sub 4:00 Miler" not "A Sub 4:00 Mile" stating that he has joined the sub 4 minute club. Also the Sunday after the meet was a party and it looks like Marty was not going to run that day, but he crossed out the "no run" entry and went 5.

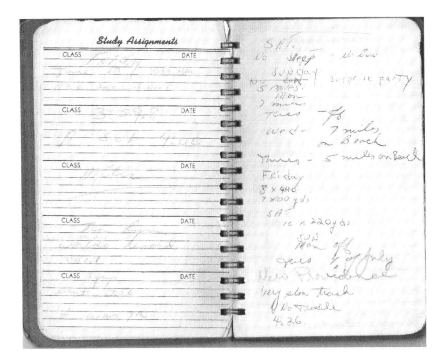

Ohio High School State Mile Champions

Jim Ryun's High School Running

This chapter is the best documentation of Jim Ryan's high school workouts and racing that we could compile from different biographies, newspaper articles and magazines. We also had the opportunity to speak with Mike Petterson, Jim Ryan's high school track team mate. Unfortunately we did not have the opportunity to interview Jim personally but we feel that the period literature used represents a very accurate log.

Jim tried out for track in junior high. He when out for the 440, the longest event. He ran a 58.5 and did not make the team. His ninth-grade year he was mustered into a 4 x 400 relay. He ran 56.4 to make the team. Jim trained for this relay by running two blocks around his house, more training than he had ever done. When he entered high school he had in mind being a quarter-mile runner on the track team.

Upon entering high school Jim attended orientation classes and heard a speech by the track and cross-country coach Bob Timmons. It was then he decided to go out for cross-country. Jim's first high school cross-country practice in early September was a half mile repeats Jim ran 2:47, 2:33, and 2:37 sat out the next two and then ran the last one in 2:40. Two days later he ran eight mile repeats at 5:40 pace. Jim started training in the mornings that first season of cross-country. The first time trial Jim finished last man on the B team. He was running 10 to 15 miles a day along with everybody else on the team. On September 14 Jim ran his first two-mile cross-country race and finished with a time of 12:11. Early October Jim lowered that two-mile time to 11:29.1. A week later he lowered again his two-mile best to 10:36 In practice he was now running 30 quarter mile repeats, averaging each one in 75 seconds. Jim finished the first season the cross-country by coming in sixth in a dual meet with a time of 10:02 on the two-mile course.

After that first fall cross-country season Jim's next endeavor was a 50 mile hike that was part of President Kennedy's fitness program. He and a teammate ran most of the 50 miles and finished in 11 hours and 32 min.

Jim sophomore winter he did very little running and conditioning. Early March track practices began and he quickly picked up where he left off that fall running 3 mile repeats in 4.48, 4.49 and 4.45. Jim ran his first competitive mile in 4:32.4 and one week later he ran a 4:26.4 beating the reigning high school state champion in the mile. It was after this

114

race Bob Timmons's coach told Jim he could be the first four-minute mile or in high school.

Jim continued to lower his mile time. April 6th he ran a 4:21.7. Jim's speed was also beginning to improve, on May 1st he ran a 1:50 half mile. Two days later he lowered is mile PR by running a 4:16.2 a new record for high school sophomores. In practice that following week he ran a two-mile time trial in 9:20.7. Mid-May Jim won the State Mile with a time of 4:16.2. Jim continued to train after state meet and the following week he ran eight 440yd repeats at an average of 57 seconds per repeat. The week following his state title Jim ran a 4:08.2 mile with the benefit of a rabbit for the first three laps. 45 minutes after that performance on the same day Jim ran a 1:54.5 half mile.

Jim continued his interval track training pointing towards the national AAU championship in mid-summer. But his season was cut short when he cut his heel on a piece of glass running barefoot at practice on a golf course. By mid-summer Jim's 440 yard personal best was down to 50.5. Jim's practice routine during the summer consisted of waking up and delivering the paper in the morning, going to a morning workout followed by summer school followed by delivering the paper in the afternoon and then another workout. On July 22nd Jim ran a 3 mile in 14:5 3.2 and on August 2nd a two-mile in 9:28.6. A week later Jim ran the fastest two-mile ever run by a high schooler in 9:13.8.

Ryun's fall workouts his junior year. Fall of 1963

Saturday - 16 miles in one hour and 30 minutes 6.07 min. per mile on hilly roads. Pool water kicking exercises.

Sunday - 5 mile run in the park.

Monday - 3 miles in the morning, afternoon workout 20 min. warm-up jog, calisthenics, four times 120 yards, 4x60 yards, mile in 4.23, calisthenics, 3x880 at 2.45 two-minute rest, cable drills (running while tied to a fence by stretching cable), 4x440 at 69 seconds with 3 min. rest run. Warm down jog one-mile 4x220 yards, 4x60 yards, jog another mile, upper body weight workout with barbells and dumbbells. Pool kicking exercise

Tuesday - 4 miles in the morning. 6x1500m averaging 5 min. rest doing calisthenics. Six times half-mile at 2.49, two half-mile warm down, pool kicking exercise

115

Ohio High School State Mile Champions

Wednesday - 4 mile morning run. Afternoon workout four sets of the following: 8x440 at 71 seconds with 3 min. rest, last set averaged 70 seconds in between sets jog the mile for rest. Finish with pool kicking exercises.

Thursday - 3 miles in the morning. Afternoon workout; two-mile warm-up, three sets of the following: 10x220 averaging 30 seconds with 2 1/2 min. rest, in between sets did calisthenics and cable run. Two-mile warm down and pool kicking exercise

Friday - Easy day, no morning run.

Weekly total mileage 75. Undefeated in cross-country and won State Meet with a record time of 9:22.2.

The winter of Jim's junior year he continued morning and afternoon workouts. Afternoon workouts were done in a combination of outdoor tracks and the indoor track at this Wichita State University Fieldhouse. When the outdoor track was wet he would do workouts on golf courses. In February Jim's mileage increased to 16 miles a day. Most of this running was on the roads with very little speed workouts. It was psychologically a very hard winter for Jim training all by himself with no coaching allowed due to state regulations. Jim did not have any competitive indoor meets that winter other than a two-mile race in California. His goal was 9 minutes flat but he fell at the start, got up and continued and came in second to Gerry Lindgren with a time of 9:22.6.

The first week of March was the official beginning of outdoor season. Jim would start his day with morning runs of 3 to 5 miles. The afternoon workouts would go something like this. 10 times for 400yds at 71 seconds, two-minute rest. Calisthenics with dumbbells. 10 times for 400yds at 69 seconds. Calisthenics with 70 pound barbells. 10 times for 400yds at 69 seconds. Calisthenics with 33 pound weights. 10 times for 400yds at 67 seconds. Total of 10 miles for the workout.

Jim ran every day the week except Sundays and travel days.

Jim's first mile was April 4th on a flooded dirt track. He ran it in 4:33.2. His mile races that spring, in progression, were 4:21, 4.33, 4:18 and a 4:11 with a last lap of 58.7. Jim was consistently running in the low 1:50s for half miles relay legs. May 1st Jim ran a 4:09.6 mile and the following week he ran a 4:12.6 mile. On May 15th Jim ran a 4:06.4 winning the State Meet his fastest mile to date.

116

Jim continued his conditioning after state meet in preparation for invitational meets in California featuring world-class runners. His goal was to run a 4.04 mile. Jim's first open mile was in the California relays where he placed third with a time of 4:01.7. His last lap was 55 seconds and he was now in the top 75 fastest milers of all time.

Jim went back to Wichita and continued his training. The following Thursday after the California relays in Monsanto Jim ran 8x440 at 63, 57, 57, 57, 57, 55, 55, and a last repeat of 53. On June 6th Jim was back in California for Compton invitational. This race contained a number of sub four-minute milers. Jim's first split was 59.2. On the second lap he was bumped by another runner stumbled into the infield regained his balance and continued but only after everyone had passed him. His time at the half-mile was 2:01.5 and his time at the three quarters mark was 3:02.8, nine yards behind the leader. Jim had a last lap of 56 finished eighth place with a time of 3:59.0. He was now 12th on the all-time US miler list and 31st on the all-time world list.

Jim's competitive running that summer was not over. Next on the schedule was qualifying and running for the Olympic time trial in the 1500m. On June 20th Jim ran in the AAU national meet, this was the pre-qualifier to the trials. Jim finished fourth with a time of 3:39.0 equivalent to 3:56.0 mile. The following week was the US Olympic time trials in New York. Jim placed fourth with a time of 3:46.1 qualifying him for the Olympic time trials in California. His last 400m in this race was 53.3, his fastest to date.

At this point Jim had run over 4380 miles in the past 12 months averaging 12 miles a day. He would train six weeks in Wichita for the Olympic trials and he started that training by going on a family trip to Colorado. After two days adjusting to altitude Jim was logging 14 miles a day in two workouts per day. He then moved to Lawrence KS where he continued his morning runs and then afternoon workouts on the University Kansas Memorial Stadium's track. Morning workouts consisted of 6 mile run. Afternoon workouts were the following; jog a mile warm-up, do 400 yard strides, 4 x 60 yard strides, run a fast 1320 with a half-mile regard recovery jog, two 660s four-minute rest, half-mile jog, 4x330 two-minute rest, half-mile jog, six 100 yard sprints two-minute rest, 8x60 yard strides 1 min. rest. Whirlpools were typical after workouts.

Ohio High School State Mile Champions

Jim also did some hill workouts during that six-week stretch. They consisted of running up a 200 yard hill at a 25° incline four times. At one practice session Jim ran 20 quarters an average 62.5.

September 13th at the LA Coliseum was the Olympic trials. Jim finished third in the 1500m with a time of 3:41.9. His last lap was 53.5 and he qualified for the Tokyo Olympics.

The second day in Japan at the Olympics Jim did a track workout running 20 quarters at averages 61 seconds. He then came down with a head cold/virus but continued to work out. His first qualifying race he finished fourth with a time of 3:44.4. His next race, the semifinals two days later, Jim finished in last place with time of 3:55.0 missing qualifying for the finals.

Senior year.

Due to the Olympics Jim joined the cross country team midseason and continuing his training under the new coach JD Edminston. Jim lead the cross-country team to an undefeated season and winning State. Jim ran a state course record of 9:08 bettering the old course record of 9:32.

Jim continued to train after cross-country. A few days before Christmas Jim injured his left leg. This sidelined Jim from running for six weeks and he missed the indoor track season. This was not completely detrimental in the eyes of Coach Edminston who had suggested that Jim take off two months regardless.

When Jim returned to training his new coach had him run road workouts entirely until the middle of March. At which time Jim began to do track workouts, they consisted of shorter faster intervals that under his previous coach Timmons.

Jim's performances early that spring included a 1:53.5 half-mile on a slow track and winning the state indoor mile in 4:07.2 a national high school indoor record. Three days later Jim competed in outdoor mile and ran a 4:04.4 with a last lap in 56 seconds. Mid-April Jim performed another 4:04 mile and at the same meet ran a half mile leg of a two-mile relay and covered his distance and 1:47.7. Jim again lowered the official high school mile record by running a 4:02.0 on a dirt track. Windy meets did not allow Jim an opportunity to run a sub four-minute mile. As the high school season drew to a close with the state meet in mid-May Jim's interval workouts became shorter and

118

faster. These workouts consisted of hundred yard and 220 yard repeats and very few quarter-mile repeats.

At state meet the goal was to break 4 minutes in the mile and the strategy to was to run splits that 60, 60 and 62 then run the last lap as fast as possible. His teammate Jim Peterson agreed to run rabbit for him making sure the first half-mile was done in two minutes flat, which he did. Then Jim was on his own. The wind cooperated and the gusting stopped. Jim passed the three-quarter mark in 3:02 and his final time was 3:58.3.

The first open meet of the summer California relays in Modesto jim won with a time of 3:58.1. The next race was the Compton invitational in early June. Jim finished third with a time of 3.56.8. It was his fastest mile and a new high school record. He moved to 11th on the all-time list the fastest milers. Jim's next meet was the AAU nationals at the end of June in San Diego.

Jim went back to Wichita to prepare for the AAU meet performing some of his hardest workouts. One of which was 20 quarter miles averaging 59 seconds the last one in 56 seconds.

Returning to California June 19th Jim ran in the high school only Golden West Invitational. He doubled up winning the two-mile in 9:04.0 and the mile and 4:04.3 with the last lap of 54 seconds. The following week Jim ran a 3 mile in 13:54 a new high school three-mile record.

The following weekend was the AAU Nationals. That Monday Jim had a hard workout but Tuesday and Wednesday were easy days. Jim qualified for the finals running a 4:11.1 and won the final in 3:55.3 with a last lap in 53.9. He set a new American record, moving up to fourth on the all-time miler list.

Spring Track Workouts Senior Year

Day	AM	PM	Non Running
Sunday		10 miles at 6:30 pace	Calisthenics
Monday	5 miles at 6:30 pace	1 x 2miles @ 9:55	Calisthenics
		2 x 1mile @ 5:15 rest 8min	Dumbells
		3 x 880 @ 3:30 rest 6	Weights

119

Ohio High School State Mile Champions

		min	
		6 x 440 @ 64 rest 3min	Light weights
		Jog 4 miles	
Tuesday	6 miles	6 x 440 @ 64 rest 3min	Calisthenics
		1 x 1320 stride	
		10 x 140 @ 18 rest 2min	Weights 5x3 drill rst 6 min
		5 x 220 @ 31 rest 2.5 min	
		1 mile warm down	
Wedesday	3 miles	20 x 440 @ 71 rest 3 min	Dumbbells
		10 x 440 @ 69 rest 3 min	Weights
		10 x 440 @ 69 rest 3 min	Light Weigths
		10 x 440 @ 69 rest 3 mi7	
Thursday	4 miles	1 mile jog	Calisthenics
		6x 880 @ 2:52 rest 6 min	Calisthenics
		6x 880 @ 2:53 rest 6 min	Calisthenics
		6x 880 @ 2:44 rest 6 min	Calisthenics
		1.5 miles	
Friday	4 miles	1760, 1320, 880, 660, 440 rest 10 min	
		3 mile x-country run	Weights
Saturday	1 mile race 4:33.2	Dirt track flooded/muddy	

Tapering
Workouts Two Weeks Before First Sub 4 Minute Mile

Day	AM	PM	Non Running
Sunday	6 miles		
Monday	5 miles		
		1 x 1mile jog	
		4 x 120, 4 x 60 WIndsprints	
		1 x 2 mile @ 9:30	
		Jog 4 miles	
Tuesday	2 miles stride	1 x 880 jog	Calisthenics
	1 mile fartlek	1 x 1 mile jog	Calisthenics
	2 miles stride	4 x 120, 4 x 60 WIndsprints	
		1 x 880 @ 2:01	
		1 mile stride	
		8 x 140 on the grass	
		1 x 880 @ 1:59	
		10 x 100	
		1 mile stride	
Wedesday	4 miles stride	11 miles on the road	(24 x 440 planned, track flooded)
Thursday	5 miles	880 mile jog	Calisthenics
		8 x 440 @ 63,57,57,57,57,55,55,53 rest 3 min	
Friday	6 miles	1 x 880 jog	Calisthenics
		1 x 1 mile jog	Calisthenics
		4 x 120, 4 x 60 WIndsprints	
		2 x 330 rest jog 110	
		1 x 880 rest jog 880	
		3 x 440 rest 3 min	
		2 x 330 rest 3 min	
		1x 220	

121

Ohio High School State Mile Champions

		1 mile jog	
Saturday		No workout - sick	
Sunday		No workout - sick	
Monday	6 miles @ 40 mins	1 x 880 jog	Calisthenics
		1 x 1 mile jog	Calisthenics
		4 x 120, 4 x 60 WIndsprints	
		3 x 880 @ 2:02,1:58.5,1:58 rest 6 min & 660 jog	
		1 mile jog	
Tuesday	6 miles	1 x 880 jog	Calisthenics
		1 x 1 mile jog	Calisthenics
		4 x 120, 4 x 60 WIndsprints	
		4 x 440 @ 55 rest 3 min	
		1 mile jog	
Wedesday	nothing	Easy run in park	
Thursday	nothing	nothing	
Friday	nothing	Compton mile	

Tim Danielson
Chula Vista High School - 1966

The second high schooler to break the 4 minute mile, Tim's effort might be the most impressive of all. Tim did not have the benefit of a world class coach in high school like Timmons or Dywer. Nor did Tim have the year around structure and oversight of a well developed program and team. Tim for the most part was out on his own. Running solo workouts in the desert hills and pacific coast beaches Tim's track accomplishments were truly his own.

As a sophomore in high school Tim played football, wrestled in the winter and baseball in the spring. As a football player he was a defensive and offensive end, and also took the field on kickoffs and punts.

Wrestling as a sophomore Tim was in the 127 pound category and was undefeated until he broke a rib during a takedown. This injury prevented him from throwing a baseball that spring, but did not prevent him from running. He joined the track team that spring as half miler. He also competed in the long jump with a best jump of 20 feet six inches.

Tim's Junior year he played varsity football, did not participate in wrestling and in the spring ran track again. After the football season, during the winter weekends he worked at a YMCA camp in the mountains east of San Diego. He worked in the kitchen and had plenty of time to run in between the meals. Tim would work out two or three times a day. Wearing cutoff jeans and leather construction work boots he would run three miles on very hilly mountain back roads. Tim would pick out hills with a 30 percent incline and do 200 yard sprints up it. He would jog back down and sprint up again repeating this 10 or more times until he could not lift his legs anymore. This is all done at an elevation of 4500 feet. Leaving the camp and returning home Mondays Tim would again train two or three times per day. His first workout was at five in the morning and he would run five miles on the roads. During these morning runs he would sprint between telephone poles that were approximately 100 yards apart.

Once a month he would not be obligated to work at the YMCA camp. During this off weekend he would continue to work out. Tim would run from his house to the ocean seven miles away. Once at the beach he would sprint from one clump of seaweed to another, picturing the distant clump of seaweeds as an imaginary finish line. Tim will run

123

approximately 2 miles on the beach performing these sprints and then run seven miles home, continuing to do sprint intervals.

Tim's junior track season he would have normal workouts Monday through Thursday and he would run two or three times per day. In the morning he would get up at 5am and run five miles with some sprints interspersed throughout typically 50 to 100 yards. Tim won the State mile his junior year with a time of 4:08.0

Tim's senior year he ran cross-country in place of football and was undefeated the whole season. After the cross-country season Tim continued to run on his own. His training was more conditioning workouts, no indoor track program was available was available to Tim.

The week before Christmas during this off-season Tim was in a toboggan accident where he broke his first and second lumbar vernier vertebrae. He was in a upper body brace for the next six weeks. It wasn't until February that he was able to start training again. Three weeks after starting to run again Tim ran a 4:11.2 mile. He finished the track season running a 4:06.2 and winning the state meet on June 4th.

At the end of his senior season Tim and his coach Harry Taylor knew that more was possible. "We figured he had the ability to break four-minute if there were other runners under four. He'd never been pushed before" recalls Taylor. Up to that point Danielson had never been in an open race and high school competition at his level did not offer him the opportunity to perform his best.

Danielson was entered in the San Diego Invitational a world class meet. The mile included top milers including Jim Ryun. That evening in Balboa Stadium, San Diego the temperature was as perfect mid-60s. "There was absolutely no wind. I could not have run that with a head wind. It was a perfect race." Recalls Tim Danielson. Balboa Stadium also had one of the first new rubberized asphalt surface. "It was very hard, but when you are only running for minutes on it, it's not that damaging. You always knew, the softer the track, the slower it was."

When the gun went off Danielson was at ease despite his lack of experience. "I really didn't think the pace was too fast," he says, "but I'll tell you, when we hit the last lap and those guys took off, I thought well this is different!" The fast competition, perfect weather and the fast track all added up and Tim came in fourth place with a time of 3:59.4.

"I remember after the race, I was really very surprised when all the people came running up to me and saying I had run under a 4 minute mile." Harry Taylor was one of the first to greet Danielson after the finish.   Tim contributes much of his success to his high school coach Harry Taylor. During practice Harry never criticize Tim or told him to slow down during his intervals training. If Tim happened to run a few seconds faster than his recommended pace, Harry would just smile and say "you must be feeling good today".

Danielson's 1966 high school state mile record:
www.youtube.com/watch?v=2-RImae6ftA

Final Thoughts

I have an ongoing debate with a football coach from my high school concerning distance running. A great guy, very successful in both his playing days and coaching career, he has been coaching since the mid 70's and has seen more than his share of high school athletes. He and I will see each other at a sporting event and start talking about standout athletes and end up on the topic of what makes a distance superstar. His thinking on the makeup of a great runner sides towards natural ability and personal drive. I come from the mind set that great runners develop from doing the right things and being well coached.

And although I have not asked him about it, I believe that my friend's bias comes from being involved in the skill sports. Football, baseball, basketball, all the sports where you either have the skill or you don't. You can hit a 70mph curveball or you can't. Things some people can do walking off the bench that others cannot do if they practiced for 100 years. Now I am not saying that great skill athletes never need to, or never do practice, they do. However, while these natural athletes can pick up a new sport in a few days or hours, no one can run a 4:30 mile after just a few runs. It does not take skill to run a 4:30 mile, it takes anaerobic conditioning over several months. Herein lies what I think is the great part of distance running. Everyone is on the same talent level to start with. Everyone has to work, work hard and work hard every day. There is no free pass.

On a deeper level I don't like the idea that someone outside the sport thinks that the top tier of distance runners are a naturally selected group. I don't like the idea of someone diminishing the reality that these people only got to their level with a lot of really tough self inflicted pain and sacrifice.

And that leads me to mention the following - that this simple exercise of determining what the winners did and following the same recipe does not mean that everyone can do this program. It takes a very self determined person that has courage, a bit of self masochism and the good fortune not to break something along the way.

Enough with the analysis. The next step is for my coaching friend and myself to pick a student out of the hallways, apply the process and watch the results. And if anyone else out there wants to play Professor Henry Higgins before I do, please let me know if Eliza Doolittle passes the test.

Supplemental Reading

Lore of Running, Fourth Edition - Tim Noakes, M.D. - 2003
The Encyclopedia of running covers everything from training, history, psychology, physiology and injuries. Almost 1000 pages on the science and sport of running. What I really like about this book is how the author constantly referenced clinical studies that show factual results not just sports stories. One of the high points of this book is the chapter on psychology where a Canadian study details the psychological traits, characteristics and methods of winners.

Daniels Running Formula - Jack Daniels, Ph.D. - 2005
The statistical bible of training and racing, times and efforts. This book is a great reference, containing page after page of data tables that are great for determining racing and work out efforts with speeds. When documenting and detailing the workout and practice routines in this book, according to our state champions, I turned a blind eye to Daniels and other existing workout routines. However, after I was finished I compared workout efforts in Daniels' book to our state champions and found them to be similar if not exactly the same on interval and tempo workout times.

The Wisdom of Crowds - James Surowiecki - 2005
Not a running or sports book, but a book that looks at the accuracy of a large group compared to that of an expert. Surowiecki reports on studies and anecdotal stories that show the average answer by a large group is more accurate than the answer of an expert. Some of this thought influenced the concept of this book.

Liquori, M., & Parker, J. L. (1980). Marty Liquori's Guide for the elite runner. Chicago, Ill: Playboy Press.

Nelson, C. (1968). The Jim Ryun story. London: Pelham Books.

Noakes, T. (2003). Lore of running. Champaign, IL: Human Kinetics.

Costill, D. L. (1979). A scientific approach to distance running. Los Altos, Calif. :: Track & Field News.

Gardner, J. B., & Purdy, J. G. (1975). Computerized running training programs. Los Altos, Calif: Tafnews Press.

Acknowledgments

The author would like to thank several people, the first being Dennis Bayham his high school coach who showed him how to train and win. Ron Russo coach at Colerain High School and Frank Russo coach at LaSalle High School both of whom have coached numerous team and individual state champions, and are always gracious with their time and knowledge. Between these two brothers they have trained five State 1600m champions in the last 15 years. The Ohio High School Athletic Association assisted greatly, always returning requests for information with emails filled with results and details.

For the third edition we have to thank Marty Liquori, Tim Danielson, Alan Webb and Mike Petterson - Jim Ryan's high school teammate. These runners not only picked up the phone and answered all my questions they also offered a lot of their own insights and even personal documents such as Marty's training log.

And finally Craig Whitmore who for decades documented the history of Ohio high school track and cross country. Craig passed away March of 2008.

About the Author

Chuck Bridgman started running track in 1973. He ran throughout grade school, high school and college. Attending Chaminade-Julienne High School in Dayton Ohio, he was coached by a state high school champion and NCAA Division I All-American. While in high school Chuck won several class AA state titles in cross country and track and set a state record. After high school, Chuck ran cross country and track for Ohio State. During the 1980's and 1990s Chuck was a registered high school track and cross country official and helped computerize the scoring for the Ohio High School State Cross Country meet. In the early nineties, Chuck started coaching cross country at Chaminade-Julienne where he aided one of his female cross country athletes in achieving multiple Division I state titles.

Contacting the Author
Please feel free to contact the author with comments or questions concerning the book at cjbridgman@gmail.com.

Ohio High School State Mile Champions

Notes:

_____

_____

_____

_____

_____

_____

_____

_____

_____

_____

_____

_____

_____

Notes:

Ohio High School State Mile Champions

Here's what they did, what they didn't do. How they trained and how they raced. No theories, no opinions. Just the facts. Just the truth.

We start in 1964 with a runner who played high school football and basketball and then set two state meet records in the mile and half mile on the same day. We'll finish in the new Jesse Owens stadium with the only runner to win three 1600m titles. In between we talk to Olympic gold medal winners and others that didn't start running track till they were juniors.

By finding out what the winners did, this book looks to answer the question, what does it takes to win the state 1600m. Workouts, dual meets, winter running, tapering, eating, weight training. What's important, what's not.

We'll try and answer the question that coaches have argued over for years; is it natural talent and will or hard work and the right program that makes a champion.

In the end we will put together a five month training routine that will produce a 4:10 1600 meter race and win you the State Division I mile.

Cover design by Stunt Chimp Enterprises
www.highschooldistancerunning.com
Published by Aardvark
Printed in USA

ISBN 978-1-4270-3458-0

51495

9 781427 634580

30851020R00079

Made in the USA
Lexington, KY
13 February 2019